Crypto Currency for Beginners Key Tips

Discover, Trade, and Grow with Crypto

By Cornelius Nathaniel Goldman

Cryptocurrency for Beginners: Key Tips

Table of Contents

Prologue

Imagine a world where your money isn't tied to a bank, where financial freedom is accessible to anyone with an internet connection. Cryptocurrency is redefining money, creating wealth and empowering individuals to control their finances in ways once thought impossible.

In this book, we'll dive into the essential knowledge you need to step confidently into this exciting digital frontier. From the most popular coins to the platforms that bring crypto to life, you'll discover how cryptocurrency works, why it's here to stay, and how you can be a part of its growing future.

Whether you're curious about Bitcoin, intrigued by Ethereum, or fascinated by the crypto revolution as a whole, this journey will show you why so many believe cryptocurrency isn't just a trend—it's a financial transformation.

Chapter 1:

Introduction to Cryptocurrency

Cryptocurrency is a revolutionary concept in today's digital world, reshaping the way we think about money and transactions. With its roots in technology and finance, cryptocurrency is as much a movement as it is a form of currency. This chapter will introduce you to the basics of cryptocurrency, explain how it differs from traditional money, and discuss the technology behind it, all while setting a positive tone about its potential and the excitement around its future.

What Is Cryptocurrency?

Cryptocurrency is a form of digital currency that relies on encryption (cryptography) to secure and verify transactions. Unlike traditional currencies, such as the U.S. dollar or the Euro, cryptocurrencies are decentralized. This means they are not issued, controlled, or regulated by any government or central bank. Instead, they exist on a global, decentralized network that is accessible to anyone with an internet connection.

Bitcoin, the first cryptocurrency, was introduced in 2009 by an anonymous individual or group called **Satoshi Nakamoto**. Designed to be a peer-to-peer electronic cash system, Bitcoin was intended to allow people to send money directly to each other without relying on banks, payment companies, or other intermediaries. Since Bitcoin's launch, thousands of other cryptocurrencies have been created, each with unique characteristics and purposes.

These digital currencies are built on a **blockchain**—a transparent and secure ledger of all transactions. Cryptocurrency, at its core, is an experiment in rethinking financial systems: can we create a form of money that doesn't require middlemen, one that operates independently of traditional financial institutions and government influence?

Why Are People So Interested in Cryptocurrency?

The growing interest in cryptocurrency is driven by a mix of technological curiosity, financial opportunity, and a desire for a more independent financial system. Here are some key reasons why people are attracted to cryptocurrency:

- **Decentralization and Independence:** Unlike bank accounts or credit systems, which are controlled and regulated by banks or governments, cryptocurrencies operate on decentralized networks. This gives users more control over their money, allowing them to store, spend, and send funds without relying on traditional institutions. For many, cryptocurrency represents a way to break free from the constraints of traditional banking.

- **Making Millionaires and Billionaires:** "Cryptocurrency has drawn interest because it has produced a surprising number of millionaires and, reportedly, even billionaires. Figures like the 'Crypto Brothers'—individuals who've famously accumulated massive wealth through crypto investments— serve as symbols of the financial potential in this emerging asset class. This success story narrative has captivated many, fueling hopes of similar gains among new and seasoned investors alike."

- **Potential for Financial Gains:** The rapid growth in the value of cryptocurrencies like Bitcoin and Ethereum has made headlines worldwide. People who bought Bitcoin for a few dollars years ago have seen it soar to tens of thousands of dollars per coin. Stories of life-changing financial gains inspire people to invest in cryptocurrency, hoping to benefit from its future growth.

- **Security and Privacy:** Transactions with cryptocurrency are often pseudonymous, meaning that while transactions are recorded, the identities behind them are private. With the blockchain's transparency and cryptographic security, users feel secure knowing their transactions are protected from tampering or fraud. For those concerned with privacy, this provides a level of protection that traditional banking often cannot.

- **Global Accessibility:** Cryptocurrency offers financial access to people in regions without stable banks or financial infrastructure. For many, it's a way to participate in the global economy, even if they don't have access to traditional financial services. This openness is particularly valuable in developing regions, where access to basic banking services may be limited.

How Cryptocurrency Differs from Traditional Money

Cryptocurrency introduces several important changes to the traditional concept of money, making it distinct in both how it works and how people use it. Here are some fundamental differences:

- **Digital-Only Form:** Cryptocurrencies exist entirely online. Unlike traditional money, which you can hold in your hand or use physically, cryptocurrencies are stored in digital wallets. Transactions are conducted through the internet, which means cryptocurrency relies heavily on technology and access to digital networks.

- **Decentralization and Control:** Traditional currencies are issued and regulated by governments and central banks. In contrast, cryptocurrencies are typically decentralized, with no single authority overseeing them. The value, creation, and management of cryptocurrencies depend on complex algorithms, peer-to-peer networks, and, in some cases, a set supply cap.

- **Scarcity and Value:** Some cryptocurrencies, like Bitcoin, have a limited supply, meaning only a fixed number of coins will ever be created. Bitcoin, for instance, is capped at 21 million coins. This scarcity can influence a cryptocurrency's value, similar to how precious metals like gold retain value because of their finite nature.

- **Transparency and Security through Blockchain:** Cryptocurrencies operate on a blockchain, a public ledger that records all transactions in a secure and tamper-proof manner. This transparency is different from traditional banks, where transaction records are kept private. Blockchain technology makes it difficult for any single entity to alter transaction records, creating trust through its security and transparency.

- **Price Volatility:** Traditional currencies are usually stable because they're supported by government policies and central banks. Cryptocurrencies, on the other hand, can be highly volatile. Their values can rise and fall dramatically within a short time, influenced by factors like news events, regulations, or social media trends.

The Technology Behind Cryptocurrency: Blockchain

Blockchain technology is the engine that powers cryptocurrencies. Think of the blockchain as a decentralized ledger, or a database, where all cryptocurrency transactions are recorded in chronological order. Each transaction is added to a "block" of data, which is then linked to the previous block, forming a continuous chain. This chain is distributed across thousands of computers (called nodes) around the world.

The key features of blockchain include:

- **Transparency:** Since the blockchain is public, anyone can view the history of transactions, providing a level of transparency that traditional banking doesn't offer. This public access builds trust among users.

- **Immutability:** Once a transaction is recorded on the blockchain, it's nearly impossible to alter or delete. This immutability is a safeguard against fraud and manipulation, making it especially useful for a currency system where trust is essential.

- **Security:** Blockchain uses advanced cryptographic techniques to secure transactions. Each block in the chain contains a unique code (a cryptographic hash) that links it to the previous block. Any attempt to alter the data would break the chain, signaling tampering. This security layer makes cryptocurrency one of the most secure systems for digital transactions.

The Rise of Bitcoin: Cryptocurrency's Beginning

Bitcoin was the first cryptocurrency, and it remains the most well-known and valuable. Launched in 2009, Bitcoin was designed as a response to the 2008 financial crisis, when trust in traditional financial institutions was at an all-time low. Bitcoin aimed to be a currency that anyone could use without needing permission from banks or governments.

Bitcoin's open-source model inspired the development of thousands of other cryptocurrencies, each seeking to improve upon or differentiate itself from Bitcoin. **Ethereum**, for example, introduced the concept of "smart contracts," allowing for programmable transactions, while **Litecoin** aimed to provide faster transaction times. Today, the cryptocurrency market includes a wide range of coins, each offering unique features, technologies, and use cases.

The Potential of Cryptocurrency: What's Next?

As cryptocurrency continues to evolve, it's hard to predict exactly where it will go. But its impact on finance, technology, and global markets is undeniable. Here are a few areas where cryptocurrency might play a major role in the future:

- **Decentralized Finance (DeFi):** DeFi platforms offer financial services without traditional banks. With DeFi, people can lend, borrow, and earn interest on their assets directly, using blockchain technology.

- **Cross-Border Payments:** Traditional cross-border transactions can be slow and expensive due to bank fees and currency exchange rates. Cryptocurrencies could provide a faster, more affordable solution for international payments.

- **Digital Identity and Privacy:** Some cryptocurrency projects aim to give people control over their digital identities, enhancing privacy and reducing reliance on centralized platforms for managing personal data.

- **Smart Contracts and Automation:** Beyond currency, blockchain technology supports smart contracts—self-executing agreements that automatically enforce terms when certain conditions are met. This has implications for everything from real estate transactions to legal agreements.

Closing Thoughts

Cryptocurrency represents a bold step into the future of finance, combining technology and economic principles in a way that could reshape our understanding of money. As you explore this book, you'll gain insight into the benefits, challenges, and applications of cryptocurrency in daily life. Whether you're a complete beginner or someone looking to expand your knowledge, this guide will empower you to make informed decisions about cryptocurrency.

Chapter 2:

Top 10 Most Popular Cryptocurrencies

Cryptocurrency has diversified significantly since Bitcoin's inception in 2009. While Bitcoin remains the most well-known, many other cryptocurrencies have emerged with distinct purposes, communities, and technological innovations. This chapter dives into the ten most popular cryptocurrencies, examining what makes each unique, how they function, and why they've gained so much attention.

1. Bitcoin (BTC)

Launch Year: 2009
Creator: Satoshi Nakamoto
Purpose: Peer-to-peer digital currency, store of value

Overview: Bitcoin is the first cryptocurrency and continues to lead the industry as both the most valuable and widely recognized digital currency. Created in the wake of the 2008 financial crisis, Bitcoin was intended to provide a decentralized alternative to traditional financial systems, allowing people to transfer funds directly to each other without a bank or intermediary.

Bitcoin's fixed supply of 21 million coins gives it scarcity, similar to precious metals like gold. This scarcity, combined with its decentralized nature, has led to Bitcoin's reputation as "digital gold," making it a preferred asset for long-term investment and wealth preservation. Bitcoin's widespread acceptance and adoption by large institutions have also bolstered its credibility, with some companies now accepting it as payment.

Bitcoin's success has inspired a wave of new cryptocurrencies, but it remains the gold standard, representing nearly half of the total crypto market cap. Its role as a store of value and hedge against inflation continues to attract interest, especially from investors and institutions.

2. Ethereum (ETH)

Launch Year: 2015
Creator: Vitalik Buterin
Purpose: Decentralized platform for applications, smart contracts

Overview: While Bitcoin paved the way for digital currencies, Ethereum revolutionized the space by introducing smart contracts—self-executing agreements that run on the blockchain. Smart contracts make Ethereum much more than a currency; it's a platform for creating decentralized applications, or dApps, which function without needing a third party to enforce terms or manage data.

Ethereum's flexibility has made it the foundation for many blockchain-based innovations, including decentralized finance (DeFi) projects, non-fungible tokens (NFTs), and a range of other applications that extend beyond finance. Ethereum has a massive developer community constantly building new applications, ensuring its relevance in the evolving crypto space.

Ethereum is currently undergoing a major upgrade called **Ethereum 2.0**, which will transition it from a proof-of-work to a proof-of-stake system, aiming to reduce energy consumption and increase transaction speeds. This transition is widely anticipated and expected to strengthen Ethereum's position as the leading smart contract platform.

3. Tether (USDT)

Launch Year: 2014
Creator: Tether Limited
Purpose: Stablecoin pegged to the U.S. dollar

Overview: Tether is the first stablecoin, a type of cryptocurrency designed to maintain a stable value by pegging itself to a traditional currency, in this case, the U.S. dollar. For every Tether token issued, the company claims to hold an equivalent amount in reserves to back it, keeping its value close to $1.

Stablecoins like Tether play a crucial role in the crypto market by offering a less volatile asset for traders who want to "park" their funds temporarily without cashing out to traditional currency. Tether is widely used in trading, DeFi, and as a bridge between different cryptocurrencies, making it one of the most transacted cryptocurrencies by volume.

Despite its widespread use, Tether has faced scrutiny regarding its reserves and transparency. Regulatory bodies continue to monitor stablecoins, but Tether remains a cornerstone of the crypto ecosystem, enabling a stable medium for traders to move funds.

4. Binance Coin (BNB)

Launch Year: 2017
Creator: Binance
Purpose: Utility token for the Binance platform and ecosystem

Overview: Binance Coin, or BNB, started as a way to give users discounted trading fees on Binance, one of the world's largest cryptocurrency exchanges. However, BNB's use has expanded significantly. Today, BNB can be used within the Binance ecosystem to pay for various transaction fees, participate in token sales, and even for transactions in certain third-party apps.

BNB is also integral to the **Binance Smart Chain (BSC)**, a blockchain launched by Binance that offers a faster and cheaper alternative to Ethereum for developers and users. The Binance ecosystem, which includes DeFi projects, NFT marketplaces, and more, has grown substantially, and BNB's utility has grown along with it, making it one of the top five cryptocurrencies by market cap.

5. USD Coin (USDC)

Launch Year: 2018
Creator: Circle and Coinbase
Purpose: Stablecoin pegged to the U.S. dollar

Overview: USD Coin, or USDC, is another stablecoin similar to Tether, aiming to maintain a value equal to the U.S. dollar. Backed by fully transparent reserves held by regulated U.S.-based institutions, USDC provides transparency and reliability, which many users find reassuring. With regular audits and collaborations with financial authorities, USDC has earned trust as one of the more stable stablecoins in the market.

USDC is widely used in the DeFi space for lending, borrowing, and other financial services where stability is essential. It's especially popular in the United States, where regulatory oversight on stablecoins is increasingly strict. Its popularity is bolstered by its association with major American companies, Circle and Coinbase.

6. Ripple (XRP)

Launch Year: 2012
Creator: Ripple Labs
Purpose: Payment protocol and cryptocurrency for cross-border payments

Overview: Ripple is unique in the crypto world because it's both a digital currency (XRP) and a global payment protocol (RippleNet) for fast, low-cost cross-border transactions. Ripple is different from most cryptocurrencies because it's not fully decentralized; Ripple Labs holds a significant portion of XRP, which has led to some controversy within the crypto community.

Ripple's partnerships with major banks and financial institutions have given it significant traction in the global payments industry. Ripple's technology can process thousands of transactions per second, making it much faster than Bitcoin. Despite its ongoing legal challenges with the U.S. Securities and Exchange Commission (SEC), XRP remains a key player in the cryptocurrency space, particularly for international payments.

7. Cardano (ADA)

Launch Year: 2017
Creator: Charles Hoskinson

Purpose: Platform for dApps and smart contracts, focusing on sustainability and scalability

Overview: Cardano is a blockchain platform built on a rigorous scientific foundation, with a focus on creating a sustainable and scalable ecosystem for decentralized applications. Cardano's unique approach to development—relying on peer-reviewed research and a proof-of-stake consensus model—sets it apart from other platforms.

Cardano's design aims to make it a more energy-efficient and scalable blockchain, tackling issues of scalability and environmental impact. Its roadmap includes a series of upgrades that will add smart contract functionality and other features to compete with Ethereum and other smart contract platforms. Cardano's growing community and commitment to sustainable technology have earned it a solid place in the top 10 cryptocurrencies.

8. Solana (SOL)

Launch Year: 2020
Creator: Anatoly Yakovenko
Purpose: High-performance blockchain for dApps, NFTs, and DeFi

Overview: Solana is a blockchain known for its high-speed transactions and low fees, capable of processing thousands of transactions per second, thanks to a unique consensus mechanism called Proof of History (PoH). This efficiency has made Solana a preferred platform for decentralized applications, particularly in the fields of DeFi and NFTs.

Solana's rapid adoption and expanding ecosystem have made it one of the most promising Ethereum alternatives. Many developers are attracted to its scalability and cost-effectiveness, and its user base continues to grow as new projects and applications are launched.

9. Dogecoin (DOGE)

Launch Year: 2013
Creators: Billy Markus and Jackson Palmer
Purpose: Originally created as a joke, now used for tipping and donations

Overview: Dogecoin began as a joke but has since evolved into a widely recognized cryptocurrency with a strong community. Known for its lighthearted culture and supportive fanbase, Dogecoin is often used for online tipping, donations, and small transactions. While Dogecoin lacks the technical complexity of other coins, its affordability and community-driven approach make it accessible to beginners.

Dogecoin's price has been influenced by endorsements from public figures, most notably Elon Musk, who has praised its potential as a "people's currency." While its use cases are limited, Dogecoin's loyal community has helped it gain significant traction.

10. Polkadot (DOT)

Launch Year: 2020
Creator: Gavin Wood

Purpose: Multi-chain platform for connecting different blockchains

Overview: Polkadot is a unique blockchain designed to connect multiple blockchains into one cohesive network. By enabling different blockchains to share data and communicate, Polkadot aims to create an "internet of blockchains." This interoperability and scalability allow various networks to work together more efficiently, reducing congestion and increasing functionality across blockchain networks.

Polkadot's architecture has attracted projects looking to leverage its connectivity, making it a key player in blockchain infrastructure. Its multi-chain design is especially promising for the future of decentralized finance, gaming, and other industries that rely on multiple interconnected applications.

Closing Thoughts

These ten cryptocurrencies represent the diversity and innovation within the cryptocurrency ecosystem. Each one serves a different purpose, from Bitcoin's store of value to Ethereum's programmable contracts, and from stablecoins like Tether to high-speed solutions like Solana. By understanding these key players, you gain insight into how the cryptocurrency landscape functions and the variety of roles digital assets can play.

Keep in mind that there are numerous other cryptocurrencies to consider. While the top ten are often more stable, established, and secure, their higher costs may make them less ideal as a starting point for beginners.

Chapter 3:

Types and Functions of Cryptocurrencies

Cryptocurrencies have grown far beyond their original role as a form of digital money, evolving into a variety of asset types, each with specific functions and purposes. Today, thousands of cryptocurrencies serve different roles, from facilitating payments and enabling decentralized applications to representing ownership in assets and giving users voting power. This chapter breaks down the main types of cryptocurrencies, providing insight into what each one does, why it matters, and how it contributes to the diverse crypto ecosystem.

1. Payment Coins

Payment coins, often called **digital cash**, were the first type of cryptocurrency created. They aim to offer a fast, secure, and decentralized way to transfer value between people or businesses, regardless of their location. These coins are the closest equivalent to traditional money in the crypto world and were developed as an alternative to bank-controlled transactions.

Examples of Payment Coins:

- **Bitcoin (BTC):** The first and most well-known cryptocurrency, Bitcoin was designed as a peer-to-peer digital currency that doesn't rely on any bank or government.

Bitcoin's success paved the way for thousands of other cryptocurrencies and established a new form of "digital gold," used for both payments and as a store of value.

- **Litecoin (LTC):** Often referred to as "the silver to Bitcoin's gold," Litecoin was developed to process transactions more quickly and affordably than Bitcoin. It remains popular for smaller transactions due to its lower fees and faster transaction speeds.

- **Bitcoin Cash (BCH):** Created in 2017 as a fork from Bitcoin, Bitcoin Cash increased the block size limit to handle a greater number of transactions, making it better suited for day-to-day payments.

How Payment Coins Work:

Payment coins operate on decentralized networks, usually with a **proof-of-work** or **proof-of-stake** consensus mechanism to verify transactions. These networks allow users to send payments directly to each other without intermediaries. Each transaction is recorded on a blockchain, making it transparent and tamper-resistant.

Benefits of Payment Coins:

- **Borderless Payments:** Payment coins allow for transactions across borders without requiring currency exchange or high international transfer fees.

- **Reduced Transaction Costs:** Transactions often cost significantly less than traditional payment methods, especially for large or international transfers.

- **Financial Inclusion:** Payment coins provide a way for people without access to traditional banking to engage in digital commerce and transactions.

Challenges and Limitations:

Payment coins face challenges with scalability, as the number of users and transactions grows, causing networks to slow down or fees to rise. Innovations like the **Lightning Network** for Bitcoin aim to address this by enabling faster, low-cost transactions off-chain, but scalability remains a central challenge.

2. Stablecoins

Stablecoins address the challenge of price volatility, one of the most significant hurdles to using cryptocurrency as a reliable currency. These cryptocurrencies are pegged to stable assets like the U.S. dollar, gold, or a basket of assets to maintain a consistent value. Stablecoins have become a critical part of the crypto market, providing a safe place to store value and facilitating seamless transitions between volatile cryptocurrencies and stable assets.

Examples of Stablecoins:

- **Tether (USDT):** One of the oldest and most widely used stablecoins, Tether is pegged to the U.S. dollar and is backed by a mix of fiat reserves and other assets.

- **USD Coin (USDC):** Created by Circle and Coinbase, USDC maintains its peg through regular audits, transparency, and regulatory compliance, making it one of the most trusted stablecoins.

- **Dai (DAI):** DAI is a decentralized stablecoin that's algorithmically pegged to the U.S. dollar. Unlike centralized stablecoins, DAI uses smart contracts to keep its value stable, backed by collateral in the MakerDAO ecosystem.

How Stablecoins Work:

Stablecoins can be backed by fiat currency, commodities, or even other cryptocurrencies. Some are **collateralized**, meaning they hold reserves in cash or assets to support each coin in circulation. Others are **algorithmically stabilized**, where smart contracts adjust the supply to maintain the peg to the target currency.

Benefits of Stablecoins:

- **Reduced Volatility:** By maintaining a stable value, stablecoins make it easier for users to store value without the risk of sudden price swings.

- **Flexible Digital Payments:** Stablecoins allow for fast, low-cost transactions without the need to convert to traditional currency.

- **Widely Used in Decentralized Finance (DeFi):** Stablecoins are crucial in DeFi applications for lending, borrowing, and earning interest.

Challenges and Controversies:

Stablecoins, especially those with fiat backing, face regulatory scrutiny over transparency and reserve requirements. Some stablecoins have come under fire for not providing sufficient proof of reserves, which raises concerns about their stability during market stress.

3. Utility Tokens

Utility tokens are created to serve a specific function within a blockchain ecosystem. They allow users to access features, pay for services, or earn rewards within that ecosystem. Unlike payment coins, utility tokens aren't meant to act as a store of value; instead, they serve as access points to decentralized applications (dApps) or platforms.

Examples of Utility Tokens:

- **Binance Coin (BNB):** Originally created to provide discounts on Binance trading fees, BNB is now used across the Binance ecosystem, including the Binance Smart Chain, which hosts DeFi and NFT applications.

- **Chainlink (LINK):** Used in the Chainlink network, LINK tokens pay for services that connect smart contracts with real-world data, bridging the gap between blockchains and external information.

- **Filecoin (FIL):** Users on the Filecoin network use FIL tokens to pay for decentralized file storage, allowing them to store data securely and privately on a distributed network.

How Utility Tokens Work:

Utility tokens are issued by specific platforms, projects, or networks, and users typically acquire them by purchasing, earning, or exchanging other cryptocurrencies for them. These tokens often have limited functionality outside of their respective ecosystems, meaning their value is tied to the success and adoption of the platform.

Benefits of Utility Tokens:

- **Access to Services:** Utility tokens enable access to specific services within a platform, making them an integral part of ecosystems like decentralized finance or gaming.

- **Incentives for Engagement:** Many projects use utility tokens to reward users for participation, building community and loyalty.

- **Flexible Applications:** Utility tokens are used in diverse applications, from cloud storage to prediction markets, allowing developers to create innovative products.

Limitations of Utility Tokens: Since utility tokens are linked to specific projects, their value depends on the platform's success. If the platform fails to gain traction, the token's utility (and price) can decrease, leading to significant investment risks.

4. Security Tokens

Security tokens represent ownership in an asset, company, or project, similar to stocks or bonds in traditional finance. These tokens must comply with securities regulations, and they're subject to oversight by regulatory bodies. Security tokens often represent real-world assets, such as equity in a company, real estate, or investment funds.

Examples of Security Tokens:

- **tZERO (TZROP):** A security token that represents ownership in the tZERO trading platform, providing investors with potential returns based on its performance.

- **RealT Tokens:** These tokens represent fractional ownership of real estate properties, enabling investors to gain real estate exposure through the blockchain.

How Security Tokens Work:

Security tokens operate on a blockchain and offer greater transparency and efficiency than traditional securities. They're created by issuing a token that represents a share or interest in an asset. These tokens are then traded on security token exchanges, subject to KYC (Know Your Customer) and AML (Anti-Money Laundering) regulations.

Benefits of Security Tokens:

- **Liquidity for Illiquid Assets:** Security tokens allow for the fractionalization of assets like real estate, enabling people to buy, sell, or trade portions of ownership.

- **Regulatory Compliance:** Security tokens comply with securities laws, providing a framework for legal and regulated investments.

- **Transparent Ownership:** Tokenized securities make ownership records clear, accessible, and tamper-proof through blockchain.

Challenges and Limitations:

Security tokens are still in a developing phase, and their adoption is slow due to regulatory challenges. Additionally, the complexity of tokenizing assets requires both technological and legal expertise, which can be a barrier to widespread adoption.

5. Governance Tokens

Governance tokens give holders voting power in decentralized projects, allowing them to participate in critical decision-making processes. These tokens play a central role in decentralized autonomous organizations (DAOs) and other community-driven projects, where users have a say in everything from technical upgrades to operational changes.

Examples of Governance Tokens:

- **Uniswap (UNI):** As the governance token for Uniswap, one of the largest decentralized exchanges, UNI allows holders to vote on proposals such as fee structures and protocol upgrades.
- **Maker (MKR):** MKR holders participate in the governance of MakerDAO, a leading DeFi protocol, voting on issues that affect the DAI stablecoin and the ecosystem's stability.

How Governance Tokens Work:

Governance tokens are distributed to users of a platform, usually as rewards for participation or liquidity provision. Holders can then propose or vote on changes to the protocol, with each token representing a certain number of votes. Decisions are implemented if they reach a predetermined threshold of approval.

Benefits of Governance Tokens:

- **Community-Led Development:** Governance tokens allow a community to direct the project's development and maintain decentralization.

- **Aligned Interests:** Token holders are incentivized to vote in the best interests of the platform, as their token's value is tied to the project's success.

- **Flexible Governance Models:** Governance tokens enable a range of decentralized governance models, from simple voting to more complex systems with multiple layers.

Risks of Governance Tokens:

Governance tokens require active participation to be effective. If holders don't vote or remain inactive, a small group of users could gain disproportionate control, potentially undermining the project's decentralization.

6. Meme Coins

Meme coins are cryptocurrencies that started as internet jokes or memes, but they've since attracted massive followings. Despite their humorous origins, some meme coins have reached billion-dollar valuations, driven by social media hype and celebrity endorsements. While they often lack technological innovation, their community-driven approach shows the power of social influence in the crypto world.

Examples of Meme Coins:

- **Dogecoin (DOGE):** Originally created as a parody of Bitcoin, Dogecoin gained popularity through its friendly community and endorsements from public figures like Elon Musk.

- **Shiba Inu (SHIB):** Dubbed the "Dogecoin killer," Shiba Inu attracted investors for its low price and meme-driven branding, reaching a high market cap with strong community support.

How Meme Coins Work:

Meme coins typically have few technological innovations compared to other cryptocurrencies. Instead, their value relies on community support, social media momentum, and occasional endorsements from influencers. Many meme coins have large circulating supplies, which keeps individual token prices low.

Pros and Cons of Meme Coins:

Meme coins offer a fun and accessible entry point to cryptocurrency, especially for newcomers. However, they're highly speculative and subject to rapid price fluctuations, making them risky investments. While some investors have made substantial profits, others have experienced losses due to the unpredictable nature of these coins.

Final Thoughts

The cryptocurrency world is far from homogeneous. Each type of cryptocurrency—from payment coins and stablecoins to utility tokens and meme coins—serves a distinct purpose, creating a multifaceted ecosystem that goes beyond digital currency. Whether you're drawn to the stability of stablecoins, the utility of governance tokens, or the novelty of meme coins, understanding these categories will help you navigate the evolving crypto landscape with confidence.

Chapter 4:

Why Cryptocurrencies Aren't Yet Ready for Everyday Purchases

Cryptocurrencies have reshaped the financial world, promising greater control, privacy, and speed in digital transactions. However, while they offer revolutionary potential, there are still many hurdles that prevent cryptocurrencies from becoming a practical payment solution for daily expenses, such as groceries, bills, or small online purchases. This chapter provides an in-depth look at these obstacles, covering everything from transaction fees and conversion costs to the regulatory and infrastructural challenges that restrict cryptocurrencies' real-world usability.

Limited Retail and Service Provider Acceptance

For cryptocurrency to become as common as using a credit card or cash, businesses and service providers need to adopt it widely. Yet, the reality is that only a small fraction of retailers accept crypto payments. This limited acceptance makes it challenging for users to spend cryptocurrency in their daily lives, as they can't use it consistently across different merchants and services.

Why Don't Most Businesses Accept Cryptocurrency?

1. **Volatility Risks:** Cryptocurrencies like Bitcoin and Ethereum experience significant price swings. For example, the value of

Bitcoin might drop by 10% within a day. A business accepting crypto could suffer losses if the coin's value decreases shortly after receiving payment. This risk makes businesses wary of holding onto crypto, especially for low-margin industries.

2. **Lack of Payment Processing Infrastructure:** Traditional payment systems like Visa, Mastercard, and PayPal are deeply embedded in the global economy, supported by almost every retail outlet. Cryptocurrency lacks the same infrastructure, which would require retailers to install new software, integrate new systems, and train staff. Many retailers don't see enough demand for crypto to justify these additional steps.

3. **Regulatory Ambiguity:** Regulations around cryptocurrency are still evolving. Many businesses fear potential legal liabilities if they handle crypto payments without fully understanding tax obligations, anti-money laundering (AML) requirements, or customer due diligence (CDD) standards. Without clear regulatory guidelines, businesses may view cryptocurrency payments as risky.

Early Adopters and Crypto Acceptance Success Stories

Some companies, especially in the tech and e-commerce sectors, have begun accepting cryptocurrency to meet demand from crypto users:

- **Microsoft:** Accepts Bitcoin for certain digital content purchases.

- **Overstock:** Allows users to buy products using Bitcoin and has seen positive feedback from the crypto community.

- **PayPal:** While not a retailer, PayPal allows users to buy, hold, and use cryptocurrency for payments, providing a bridge for crypto use with millions of merchants in its network.

These companies reflect an encouraging start, but true mainstream adoption is far from reality. Widespread acceptance will require not only greater technological integration but also regulatory clarity and more stable crypto prices.

High Transaction Fees and Conversion Costs

Cryptocurrencies are often promoted as a cost-effective way to transfer money. However, transaction fees, conversion costs, and additional expenses can sometimes make small, everyday transactions impractical. These costs vary significantly depending on the cryptocurrency, network congestion, and the size of the transaction.

Types of Costs Involved in Crypto Transactions

1. **Network Fees (Gas Fees):** Many cryptocurrencies require users to pay network fees, also known as "gas fees" on networks like Ethereum, to process transactions. These fees can fluctuate based on network congestion. For instance, during times of high demand, such as the launch of a popular decentralized finance (DeFi) application, gas fees can skyrocket. While this may be manageable for high-value transactions, it makes small purchases, like a cup of coffee, disproportionately expensive.

2. **Conversion Fees on Exchanges:** If users need to convert their crypto into traditional currency, they usually need to go through an exchange, which often charges a conversion fee. These fees can range from 0.1% to several percentage points, depending on the exchange. For frequent transactions, these conversion fees can accumulate quickly.

3. **Exchange Fees and Spread:** Beyond conversion fees, exchanges may charge fees for trading, withdrawals, and deposits. Additionally, exchanges sometimes impose hidden costs through spread (the difference between buy and sell prices), which can impact the effective rate users receive when cashing out their crypto.

4. **Crypto ATM Fees:** Some crypto ATMs allow users to withdraw cash by converting crypto, but these machines often charge fees of 10-15%. For example, withdrawing $100 from a crypto ATM may cost an additional $10 or more, making it impractical for frequent use.

Examples of Crypto Network Fees and Their Impact on Small Purchases

- **Bitcoin Fees:** Bitcoin transactions are validated through a process called proof-of-work, which can be slow and costly during times of high demand. Fees can range from a few dollars to over $20 per transaction. Paying $20 to buy a $5 item is obviously inefficient, making Bitcoin impractical for daily purchases.

- **Ethereum's Gas Fees:** Due to Ethereum's popularity for decentralized applications, its network often experiences congestion, causing gas fees to rise. During peak periods, gas

36

fees can cost more than $50 per transaction, rendering Ethereum unusable for small transactions.

These fees are a significant barrier to everyday crypto use. For crypto to become a practical payment option, transaction costs will need to be reduced to levels comparable with traditional financial systems. Several solutions, such as **layer-2 scaling** (e.g., the Lightning Network for Bitcoin) and **proof-of-stake** (Ethereum's transition to Ethereum 2.0), are being developed to address this, but widespread adoption is still in progress.

Complex Process of Converting Crypto to Cash

Unlike traditional money in a bank account, converting crypto to cash involves several steps that can be both time-consuming and costly. This process is necessary because few places accept direct crypto payments, meaning users need to exchange their crypto holdings for fiat currency (e.g., dollars or euros) to make traditional purchases.

Typical Steps to Convert Crypto to Cash

1. **Selling Crypto on an Exchange:** Most people use cryptocurrency exchanges, like Coinbase, Binance, or Kraken, to sell their crypto holdings. This requires creating an account, verifying identity, and linking a bank account.

2. **Waiting for Transaction Confirmation and Bank Processing:** Once crypto is sold, it can take several days to transfer the cash to a bank account. Delays are often due to exchange processing times, banking regulations, and the amount being transferred.

3. **Dealing with Daily Withdrawal Limits and Fees:**
Exchanges often impose withdrawal limits and fees, which
can make it challenging for users to convert large amounts
quickly or affordably.

Crypto ATMs: A Limited Option for Cash Conversion

Crypto ATMs offer an alternative to online exchanges but come
with several limitations:

- **Geographic Limitations:** Crypto ATMs are mainly located
  in urban areas, limiting access for people in smaller towns or
  rural regions.

- **High Fees:** As mentioned, crypto ATMs often charge high
  fees, which can range from 5-20% of the withdrawal amount,
  making them an impractical solution for regular use.

- **Limited Withdrawal Amounts:** Many crypto ATMs cap the
  amount of cash users can withdraw in a single transaction,
  restricting their usefulness for larger cash needs.

The inability to easily convert cryptocurrency into cash limits its
flexibility and convenience, reducing its practicality as a day-to-
day currency.

Difficulty Paying Bills and Everyday Services with Crypto

A future where users can pay for rent, electricity, groceries, or
streaming subscriptions directly with cryptocurrency remains a
goal, but it's still out of reach. Although some service providers
and niche platforms accept crypto, the overall acceptance rate is

low, and logistical challenges prevent crypto from being a viable option for bill payments.

Challenges in Paying Bills with Crypto

1. **Inconsistent Payment Processing Times:** Unlike traditional bank transactions, which are generally instant, cryptocurrency transactions can vary widely in processing speed. For example, Bitcoin transactions can take anywhere from 10 minutes to an hour, and Ethereum can be similarly inconsistent, depending on network congestion.

2. **Need for Third-Party Conversion Services:** Companies like BitPay and CoinPayments offer solutions for bill payments in crypto by converting digital currency to fiat for merchants. However, these services often charge additional fees, and users are still subject to tax and reporting requirements for each transaction.

3. **Lack of Direct Acceptance by Essential Service Providers:** Although some companies and industries have started accepting crypto, essential services (e.g., utility companies, insurance providers, and healthcare providers) typically don't. For these companies, the complexity, legal liabilities, and tax implications are deterrents that outweigh any demand from customers to pay in crypto.

Real-World Examples of Crypto Bill Payment Solutions

- **BitPay:** BitPay is one of the most prominent crypto payment processors and offers bill payment solutions. However, while BitPay allows users to pay with crypto, the recipient still receives traditional currency, meaning the user technically isn't paying directly in crypto.

- **CoinPayments:** Another service that enables businesses to accept cryptocurrency payments, CoinPayments allows users to pay for certain goods and services, but it's mostly limited to online or crypto-focused merchants.

These services represent a step forward, but the infrastructure is not yet developed enough to support direct, widespread bill payment with crypto.

Tax and Regulatory Complications

Using cryptocurrency for daily purchases is often complicated by tax and regulatory requirements. In many countries, each crypto transaction is treated as a capital gain or loss, creating a tax event that must be reported, regardless of the transaction amount.

Capital Gains Taxes on Crypto Transactions

In the United States and many other countries, cryptocurrency is treated as property for tax purposes. This means that whenever crypto is used to make a purchase, the difference between the purchase price and the current value at the time of sale must be reported as a capital gain or loss. For small transactions, this requirement is cumbersome and creates additional paperwork:

- **Example of a Taxable Transaction:** If a user buys Bitcoin for $1,000 and then uses it to make a $500 purchase when the Bitcoin's value has risen to $2,000, the user incurs a $500 capital gain (the difference between $1,000 and $1,500). This gain must be reported and potentially taxed.

Income Reporting Requirements

In countries where crypto is regulated, individuals are required to report all cryptocurrency transactions, including buying, selling, and even using crypto for purchases. This can create a complex administrative burden for those who want to use crypto regularly, as every transaction must be documented for tax purposes.

Differences in Regulatory Approaches Across Countries The regulatory landscape for cryptocurrency varies significantly between countries:

- **El Salvador:** The first country to adopt Bitcoin as legal tender, enabling citizens to use it for a variety of payments. However, challenges remain in terms of infrastructure and financial stability.

- **China:** Has banned most cryptocurrency activities, making it difficult for residents to use or transact in crypto.

- **European Union and United States:** Both regions have detailed tax and reporting regulations for crypto, requiring individuals and businesses to keep track of all transactions for tax purposes.

This regulatory complexity discourages many from using crypto for everyday purchases, as it requires meticulous record-keeping and exposes them to potential tax liabilities.

Stablecoins: A Potential Solution for Everyday Transactions

Stablecoins, such as **Tether (USDT)** and **USD Coin (USDC)**, offer a promising alternative for those looking to use cryptocurrency without the volatility of traditional assets. Pegged to stable assets, like the U.S. dollar, stablecoins maintain a predictable value, which could make them more practical for everyday purchases.

Benefits of Using Stablecoins for Purchases

- **Reduced Volatility:** Stablecoins maintain a consistent value, making them suitable for transactions where price stability is important.

- **Lower Fees:** Some blockchains supporting stablecoins have lower transaction fees, especially on networks optimized for stablecoin transfers, like Binance Smart Chain.

- **Increased Acceptance in DeFi and Certain Retailers:** Stablecoins are widely used in decentralized finance (DeFi) applications, and some merchants that accept crypto now include stablecoins as a payment option.

Limitations and Challenges of Stablecoins

- **Regulatory Concerns:** Stablecoins face increasing scrutiny from regulators, who worry about their impact on the stability of traditional currencies. Changes in regulation could impact their usability for everyday transactions.

- **Limited Adoption in Traditional Retail:** While stablecoins have gained popularity within the crypto ecosystem, they are still not widely accepted outside of it.

Emerging Solutions:

Crypto Debit Cards and Payment Processors

Several companies have launched crypto debit cards and payment processors to make it easier for people to spend crypto in real-world settings. These solutions offer a bridge between cryptocurrency and traditional finance, allowing users to spend crypto without the typical conversion process.

Crypto Debit Cards Crypto debit cards, offered by companies like **Coinbase**, **Crypto.com**, and **Binance**, enable users to load their crypto balance onto a card and spend it like fiat currency. The crypto is automatically converted to traditional money at the time of purchase, allowing users to pay merchants who don't accept crypto directly.

Advantages of Crypto Debit Cards

- **Instant Conversion:** Crypto debit cards convert crypto to fiat currency instantly at the point of sale, making it easy to use crypto with regular businesses.

- **Widespread Merchant Acceptance:** Since these cards operate on major networks like Visa or Mastercard, they are accepted at millions of merchants worldwide.

Challenges of Crypto Debit Cards

- **High Fees and Conversion Rates:** Crypto debit cards often include hidden costs, such as conversion fees, foreign transaction fees, and ATM fees.

- **Limited Crypto Options:** Some crypto debit cards only support a few major cryptocurrencies, limiting flexibility for users with diverse portfolios.

Crypto Payment Processors

Payment processors like **BitPay** and **CoinPayments** provide businesses with a way to accept crypto by instantly converting it to fiat currency. These services make it easier for businesses to accept crypto without exposure to price volatility.

Challenges with Crypto Payment Processors

- **Adoption is Still Limited:** While these services provide a practical solution, most businesses haven't integrated crypto payment processors due to limited demand and the complexity of handling crypto payments.

- **Regulatory Compliance:** Payment processors must adhere to financial regulations, which can create additional complexity for both businesses and users.

Final Thoughts

Cryptocurrency holds significant potential as a payment method, but challenges like high fees, limited merchant acceptance, regulatory burdens, and tax implications restrict its practicality. While innovations like stablecoins, crypto debit cards, and payment processors offer solutions, they are still early-stage efforts that need further development and acceptance to support widespread use.

Chapter 5:

Understanding Cryptocurrency Regulations and Taxes

As cryptocurrencies gain traction worldwide, governments are establishing frameworks to regulate and tax these digital assets. Regulations impact nearly every aspect of crypto—how it's traded, taxed, and even stored. For those new to cryptocurrency, understanding the regulatory environment and tax requirements is essential to ensure compliance and avoid potential legal or financial setbacks. In this chapter, we explore why governments regulate crypto, the different types of regulations, tax implications, and best practices for staying compliant in the evolving crypto landscape.

Why Are Governments Regulating Cryptocurrency?

Cryptocurrencies offer decentralization, privacy, and global accessibility, which challenge traditional finance and governance. Governments are interested in regulating cryptocurrency for several reasons:

1. **Tax Revenue Generation:** As crypto adoption grows, governments view it as a potential revenue source. Implementing tax rules allows governments to collect income and capital gains taxes on crypto transactions.

2. **Keeping Control of Money Supply:** Governments world wide do not want to lose their authority, contro, and income which is generated through central banks and financial institutions.

3. **Preventing Money Laundering and Financial Crime:** Cryptocurrencies, due to their semi-anonymous nature, can be misused for money laundering or illegal transactions. Regulations requiring user identification (KYC) and monitoring transactions (AML) are in place to prevent misuse.

4. **Consumer Protection:** The volatility and risks associated with cryptocurrency expose investors to potential scams, fraud, and significant losses. Regulations aim to protect consumers from bad actors and risky projects.

5. **Maintaining Economic Stability:** Cryptocurrencies have the potential to disrupt financial markets and traditional banking. Governments seek to balance crypto innovation with measures that protect financial stability and currency sovereignty.

Key Types of Cryptocurrency Regulations

Cryptocurrency regulations differ across countries, but they typically fall into three main categories:

1. **Tax Regulations:** These laws determine how cryptocurrency transactions are taxed. Many countries treat crypto as property (like stocks), meaning they are subject to capital gains tax. However, the specifics can vary based on transaction type, use case, and region.

2. **Trading and Exchange Regulations:** These regulations govern how exchanges operate, including requirements for KYC (Know Your Customer) and AML (Anti-Money Laundering) practices. They ensure exchanges monitor user identities and report suspicious transactions.

3. **Usage Restrictions or Bans:** Some countries restrict or ban cryptocurrency activities, including trading, mining, or certain uses. These regulations are designed to control the impact of crypto on financial stability or prevent illegal activities.

Regulatory Approaches in Key Countries

Each country has a unique stance on cryptocurrency, reflecting its financial, legal, and economic priorities. Here's an overview of how some major economies regulate crypto:

1. United States

The U.S. has a complex regulatory landscape, with multiple agencies involved, including the **Internal Revenue Service (IRS)**, **Securities and Exchange Commission (SEC)**, and **Commodity Futures Trading Commission (CFTC)**.

- **Taxation:** The IRS treats cryptocurrency as property, meaning all crypto transactions (trades, conversions, purchases) are taxable events. Each sale or trade is subject to capital gains tax, and the IRS requires users to report these transactions accurately.

- **Securities Regulation:** The SEC regulates crypto assets that qualify as securities. Many tokens sold in initial coin offerings (ICOs) fall under securities regulations and must be registered with the SEC.

- **AML and KYC Requirements:** Exchanges operating in the U.S. must follow strict KYC and AML standards, verifying user identities and monitoring transactions for suspicious activity.

Example of U.S. Taxation:

Suppose a U.S. user buys 1 Bitcoin (BTC) at $20,000, and it rises to $40,000. If they trade it for Ethereum (ETH) while the BTC price is $40,000, they would owe capital gains tax on the $20,000 increase. Each crypto-to-crypto trade is a taxable event in the U.S., which makes reporting and record-keeping essential.

2. European Union (EU)

The EU's cryptocurrency regulatory framework focuses on consumer protection and AML measures. The **Fifth Anti-Money Laundering Directive (5AMLD)** requires EU-based crypto exchanges and wallet providers to comply with KYC and AML rules.

- **Taxation:** Tax rates vary across EU countries, with most nations treating crypto as property. Some countries offer tax breaks for holding crypto long-term or exempt small transactions.

- **Proposed MiCA Framework:** The **Markets in Crypto-Assets (MiCA) Regulation** is a proposed EU regulation aimed at creating a unified approach to crypto regulation across member states. MiCA would provide legal certainty, establish investor protections, and standardize regulatory practices.

Example of EU Variance in Taxation:
In Germany, holding cryptocurrency for over a year exempts it from capital gains tax, encouraging long-term investment. In contrast, countries like France tax crypto-to-fiat conversions at a standard capital gains rate, with no long-term exemption.

3. China

China has taken one of the strictest approaches to cryptocurrency, banning nearly all crypto-related activities, including trading and mining.

- **Trading Ban:** Cryptocurrency exchanges cannot legally operate within China, and Chinese citizens are prohibited from using domestic services to trade crypto. Despite this, some individuals trade on overseas platforms using VPNs.

- **Mining Ban:** In 2021, China banned cryptocurrency mining, which caused miners to relocate to more crypto-friendly countries. The government cited financial stability and environmental concerns as reasons for the ban.

Impact of China's Restrictions:
Despite the bans, some Chinese citizens still access crypto through overseas exchanges. However, these users face significant risks, including potential fines and the lack of legal protection.

4. Japan

Japan is one of the most crypto-friendly countries, providing clear regulations that support innovation while ensuring consumer protection.

- **Legal Status:** Japan treats Bitcoin and certain other cryptocurrencies as legal property, meaning they can be used for purchases and are subject to capital gains tax.

- **FSA Oversight:** Japan's Financial Services Agency (FSA) oversees crypto exchanges, requiring them to register and follow strict AML and consumer protection practices.

Japan's Regulatory Model:

Japan's well-defined crypto laws provide a balanced approach. Japanese exchanges must meet rigorous standards, creating a trustworthy environment that encourages innovation while protecting consumers.

5. El Salvador

In 2021, El Salvador became the first country to adopt Bitcoin as legal tender, sparking international interest and debate.

- **Legal Tender Status:** Businesses in El Salvador are required to accept Bitcoin for payments, though citizens have the option to pay in USD if they prefer.

- **Risks and Incentives:** While this move aims to boost financial inclusion and reduce remittance fees, it has been criticized for exposing citizens to Bitcoin's volatility. The government offers incentives, such as Bitcoin wallets with initial funds, to encourage adoption.

El Salvador's Experiment:

El Salvador's adoption of Bitcoin as legal tender is a pioneering move, though it has faced international criticism. Some worry that the country's economy could suffer if Bitcoin's value fluctuates drastically.

Tax Implications of Cryptocurrency Transactions

Cryptocurrency tax obligations vary by country, and it's crucial for users to understand what constitutes a taxable event. In many countries, crypto transactions are subject to capital gains tax, income tax, or both.

Common Types of Taxable Crypto Events

1. **Buying and Selling:** Converting crypto to fiat currency (e.g., selling Bitcoin for USD) creates a taxable event in most countries. The capital gain (or loss) is calculated based on the difference between the purchase price and the sale price.

2. **Trading One Cryptocurrency for Another:** Exchanging one cryptocurrency for another (e.g., Bitcoin for Ethereum) is a taxable event. The gain or loss is calculated based on the difference in value at the time of the trade.

3. **Using Crypto for Purchases:** Spending crypto on goods or services is treated as a sale of property. For example, buying coffee with Bitcoin could trigger a capital gains tax, depending on the purchase and current market value.

4. **Earning Crypto as Income:** Any crypto received as payment, such as wages, freelance earnings, or mining rewards, is considered taxable income based on its fair market value at the time it's received.

Examples of Taxable Crypto Scenarios:

- **Example 1:** An investor buys Ethereum (ETH) for $1,000. A year later, it's worth $3,000, and they use it to buy a laptop. The $2,000 increase is considered a capital gain, and taxes are owed on that amount.

- **Example 2:** A freelancer is paid in Bitcoin worth $500 for a project. This income must be reported at the value of $500 on the date received, and they owe income tax on that amount.

Types of Crypto-Related Taxes

- **Capital Gains Tax:** Applies to profits made from selling, trading, or using cryptocurrency. Short-term gains (held under a year) are often taxed at a higher rate, while long-term gains may have a lower rate.

- **Income Tax:** If cryptocurrency is received as payment, it is typically subject to income tax. This includes crypto earned through mining, staking, airdrops, and as part of a salary.

- **Mining and Staking Taxes:** Crypto earned from mining or staking is often considered income, based on its fair market value at the time it's received.

Record-Keeping and Reporting Requirements

With many tax authorities treating cryptocurrency as property, accurate record-keeping is critical for compliance. Every crypto transaction must be documented, including trades, purchases, and income, to ensure accurate reporting and avoid potential penalties.

Best Practices for Crypto Record-Keeping

1. **Track All Transactions:** Record the date, type, quantity, and value of each transaction. Most exchanges provide transaction histories, which can be exported and stored for tax purposes.

2. **Maintain Documentation:** Keep records of purchase and sale confirmations, wallet addresses, and relevant statements showing the cost basis (original purchase price) and sale price.

3. **Use Crypto Tax Software:** Tools like **CoinTracking**, **CryptoTrader.Tax**, and **Koinly** help automate record-keeping, calculate gains and losses, and generate tax reports for filing.

Example of Detailed Record-Keeping

If a user buys 1 Ethereum (ETH) at $1,000, trades it for Bitcoin when it's worth $2,000, and later sells the Bitcoin at $3,000:

- **Transaction 1:** Record the ETH purchase price of $1,000.

- **Transaction 2:** Log the ETH-to-BTC trade with a value of $2,000.

- **Transaction 3:** Note the BTC sale at $3,000 and calculate total gains for tax purposes.

Good record-keeping is vital for avoiding tax discrepancies, audits, and penalties, especially for frequent traders.

Avoiding Regulatory and Tax Pitfalls

Navigating crypto regulations and taxes can be complex, but staying informed and following best practices can help you avoid potential issues.

Strategies for Regulatory and Tax Compliance

1. **Understand Local Laws and Tax Obligations:** Research the specific regulations in your country, including reporting requirements, tax obligations, and potential exemptions for long-term holdings.

2. **Use Regulated Exchanges and Wallets:** Choosing reputable, regulated platforms makes compliance easier, as they typically adhere to KYC and AML rules, and provide transaction histories.

3. **Report All Taxable Events Accurately:** Every transaction, including trades, sales, and crypto-based purchases, should be reported. Omissions can lead to penalties, audits, or legal consequences.

4. **Consult a Tax Professional:** A tax advisor experienced in cryptocurrency can help you navigate complex rules, claim deductions, and ensure full compliance.

Looking to the Future: Potential Regulatory Changes

As the cryptocurrency industry grows, regulatory frameworks are likely to evolve, possibly including:

- **Global Standards for Crypto Regulations:** Organizations like the Financial Action Task Force (FATF) are working on global standards for crypto regulations, which could help create consistency across borders.

- **Stablecoin and DeFi Oversight:** Stablecoins and decentralized finance (DeFi) applications are expected to face stricter rules to prevent misuse and ensure stability.

- **Environmental Regulations:** Environmental concerns about proof-of-work mining may lead governments to incentivize greener blockchain alternatives, such as proof-of-stake.

Final Thoughts

Cryptocurrency regulations and taxes are complex and constantly changing. For new users, understanding basic tax obligations and following best practices for reporting are crucial steps to ensuring compliance. While crypto offers freedom and flexibility, it also comes with legal responsibilities that can vary widely by region. As the industry continues to mature, clearer regulations and global standards may emerge, making it easier for users to navigate the legal landscape of crypto ownership and transactions.

Chapter 6:

Crypto Wallets: Types, Security, and Best Practices for Storing Digital Assets

Cryptocurrency, unlike traditional currency, exists entirely in digital form. To access, manage, and store it, users need a **crypto wallet**—a tool that holds the private keys necessary to interact with the blockchain and manage digital assets. A crypto wallet doesn't hold the cryptocurrency directly but stores the **digital keys** that prove ownership, enabling you to transfer, receive, and view your crypto funds.

This chapter explores the essential types of crypto wallets, security measures to protect assets, and practical advice to keep your cryptocurrency safe from theft, loss, or hacking.

Understanding Crypto Wallet Basics: Public and Private Keys

A cryptocurrency wallet operates through two essential components:

1. **Public Key:** This is a publicly shareable address, similar to an email address, that allows others to send cryptocurrency to your wallet. Public keys are safe to share, and each wallet has a unique public key associated with it.

2. **Private Key:** A private key is like a password and should never be shared. It grants access to the funds in your wallet.

Losing a private key or having it compromised means losing access to your assets.

For a user, protecting the private key is the core responsibility in crypto management. If you lose it or someone else gains access, there's no way to recover the funds from the blockchain. That's why wallet security is paramount.

Types of Crypto Wallets

Crypto wallets fall into two main categories based on how they store private keys: **cold storage wallets** and **hot storage wallets**. Cold storage wallets are offline, while hot wallets are connected to the internet, each offering different levels of security and convenience.

Let's examine the most common types of crypto wallets and their features, advantages, and drawbacks.

1. Hardware Wallets (Cold Storage)

Hardware wallets are physical devices, often resembling a USB drive, that store private keys offline. This offline status protects them from online threats such as hacking or phishing attacks, making hardware wallets one of the most secure storage methods.

Popular Hardware Wallet Brands:

- **Ledger (Nano S, Nano X):** Ledger's Nano models support a wide variety of cryptocurrencies and offer strong security.

The Nano X, with Bluetooth capabilities, is suitable for mobile users.

- **Trezor (Model One, Model T):** Trezor wallets are known for their user-friendly design, robust security, and compatibility with multiple coins.

- **KeepKey:** Known for its simplicity and affordability, KeepKey supports a narrower range of cryptocurrencies but provides a good security-to-cost balance.

How Hardware Wallets Work:

A hardware wallet keeps the private key secure within the device itself. To initiate a transaction, you connect the wallet to a computer or mobile device and confirm the transaction directly on the hardware wallet, preventing the private key from being exposed to the internet.

Security Features:

- **PIN Code and Recovery Phrase:** Most hardware wallets require a PIN code for access. During setup, they also generate a 12-24 word recovery phrase, which can restore access if the device is lost or damaged.

- **Offline Storage (Cold Storage):** Since hardware wallets are not connected to the internet unless plugged in, they are highly resistant to cyberattacks.

Pros of Hardware Wallets:

- **High Security:** Being offline most of the time, hardware wallets are immune to most online threats, including malware and hacking attempts.

- **Supports Multiple Cryptocurrencies:** Leading hardware wallets like Ledger and Trezor support hundreds of cryptocurrencies, making them versatile for diversified portfolios.

- **Backup Options:** With a recovery phrase, users can restore their wallets even if the physical device is lost or damaged.

Cons of Hardware Wallets:

- **Cost:** Hardware wallets range from $50 to $200, which can be a barrier for some users.

- **Less Convenient for Daily Use:** Hardware wallets are ideal for long-term storage rather than frequent transactions, as they require physical connection for each transaction.

- **Potential Physical Vulnerability:** If not stored securely, hardware wallets can be stolen, lost, or damaged.

Best Suited For: Long-term investors and holders with significant cryptocurrency holdings who prioritize security over convenience.

2. Software Wallets (Hot Storage)

Software wallets are digital applications or programs that store private keys on an internet-connected device, such as a smartphone, computer, or web server. These wallets offer greater convenience but come with additional security risks due to their online status.

There are three primary types of software wallets:

A. Desktop Wallets

Desktop wallets are software applications installed directly on your computer. These wallets give you full control over your private keys and typically offer a wide range of features and customization options.

- **Examples: Exodus** (user-friendly, supports multiple cryptos), **Electrum** (specializes in Bitcoin), **Atomic Wallet** (multi-crypto support).

- **Pros:** Desktop wallets provide a high level of control, are relatively secure if the computer is well-protected, and often feature an intuitive interface.

- **Cons:** Vulnerable to malware and hacking if the computer is compromised.

Best For: Users who primarily manage crypto from a desktop or laptop and can ensure good computer security.

B. Mobile Wallets

Mobile wallets are smartphone applications that make it easy to access and manage cryptocurrency on the go. With mobile wallets, users can quickly make payments, trade, and interact with decentralized applications (dApps).

- **Examples: Trust Wallet** (supports numerous cryptocurrencies), **Mycelium** (Bitcoin-focused), **Coinbase Wallet** (beginner-friendly).

- **Pros:** Highly convenient for frequent transactions, ideal for everyday use, and often feature compatibility with dApps.

- **Cons:** Dependent on phone security—vulnerable if the device is lost, hacked, or infected with malware.

Best For: Active traders or users who want to make quick transactions and need mobile accessibility.

C. Web Wallets

Web wallets are wallets accessed via a browser, often provided by exchanges or wallet providers. These wallets are popular for their ease of access and integration with trading platforms but are more susceptible to phishing and hacking.

- **Examples: MetaMask** (Ethereum and DeFi-focused), **Binance Wallet** (exchange-based), **Kraken Wallet**.

- **Pros:** Easy access from any device with internet, highly convenient for users trading on an exchange.

- **Cons:** Relies on third-party security; if the exchange or platform is hacked, funds could be at risk.

Best For: Users who need easy access for trading on exchanges or interacting with dApps but understand the higher risk of online storage.

Security Considerations for Software Wallets:

- **Two-Factor Authentication (2FA):** Many software wallets support 2FA, which adds an extra layer of security by requiring a code from a secondary device.

- **Device Security:** Since software wallets are online, they rely on the security of the device they're installed on. Users should keep devices secure with strong passwords, antivirus software, and regular updates.

Pros of Software Wallets:

- **Convenient for Frequent Access:** Software wallets are ideal for users who need frequent, fast access to their assets.

- **Support for Multiple Cryptos and dApps:** Many software wallets offer compatibility with decentralized applications and DeFi, giving users broader functionality.

Cons of Software Wallets:

- **Susceptible to Cyber Attacks:** Being online, they're more vulnerable to phishing, hacking, and malware attacks.

- **Device Dependent:** Security relies heavily on the device's security—if compromised, funds are at risk.

Best Suited For: Users who prioritize convenience and frequently use crypto for transactions, trading, or decentralized applications.

3. Paper Wallets (Cold Storage)

A **paper wallet** is a physical printout that contains a wallet's private and public keys, often in the form of QR codes. Paper wallets are a form of cold storage and offer high security as they are entirely offline. However, they come with significant physical risks.

How Paper Wallets Work:

To create a paper wallet, you generate keys using a secure tool (often a web-based generator) and print them out. Since paper wallets are entirely offline, they are immune to online hacking.

Security Considerations:

- **Use Secure Generators:** Ensure you generate paper wallets on an offline device and printer, as online access can expose keys to malware or unauthorized access.

- **Store Securely:** Paper wallets must be kept in secure locations, like a safe, to protect against physical threats such as fire, water damage, or theft.

-

Pros of Paper Wallets:

- **Offline and Immune to Hacking:** Paper wallets are cold storage, making them highly secure against digital attacks.

- **Low Cost:** Unlike hardware wallets, paper wallets are free or very low-cost, making them accessible for all users.

Cons of Paper Wallets:

- **Vulnerable to Physical Damage or Loss:** Paper is fragile and can easily be damaged, lost, or stolen. If the paper is destroyed, the funds are lost.

- **Inconvenient for Transactions:** To access funds, users must transfer assets to a software wallet, which can be cumbersome.

Best Suited For: Users seeking a highly secure, low-cost cold storage solution and are comfortable with the responsibility of managing physical storage carefully.

4. Multi-Signature Wallets (Multi-Sig)

Multi-signature wallets, or multi-sig wallets, require multiple private keys to authorize a transaction. Multi-sig wallets are often used for shared accounts or high-security accounts where single-key access is deemed too risky.

How Multi-Sig Wallets Work:

A multi-sig wallet can be set up to require multiple approvals for a transaction. For example, a 2-of-3 multi-sig wallet requires two of the three available private keys to approve a transaction.

Security Advantages of Multi-Sig Wallets:

- **Added Protection:** Multi-sig wallets reduce the risk of unauthorized access since multiple approvals are required to perform any transaction.

- **Shared Responsibility:** They are ideal for businesses or families needing shared access to funds with an added layer of security.

Best Suited For: Businesses, organizations, or families who need shared access or high-security funds.

Advanced Security Practices for Crypto Wallets

Securing your crypto wallet requires a combination of technological measures and personal practices to ensure your assets remain safe.

1. Use Strong Passwords and Enable Two-Factor Authentication (2FA)

- **Strong Passwords:** Create complex passwords with a combination of letters, numbers, and symbols. Avoid reusing passwords from other accounts.

- **Two-Factor Authentication (2FA):** Most software and web wallets support 2FA, adding an extra step for account access.

2. Protect Your Private Keys and Recovery Phrases

- **Store Offline:** Always keep private keys and recovery phrases offline, securely written down, or stored in secure physical locations (e.g., a safe).

- **Never Share or Digitize Keys:** Avoid storing keys on devices or in cloud storage, as they can be hacked or accessed remotely.

3. Regularly Backup Wallets and Recovery Phrases

- **Multiple Backups:** It's wise to keep multiple backups of recovery phrases in different secure locations.

- **Encrypted Backups for Software Wallets:** Many wallets offer encrypted backup files that can be securely stored on external devices.

4. Avoid Phishing Scams

- **Verify URLs and Emails:** Be cautious with links and emails, as phishing scams often mimic legitimate wallet providers.

- **Browser Bookmarks:** Bookmark wallet URLs to avoid typing errors or falling for fake sites.

5. Update Wallet Software and Firmware Regularly

- **Stay Updated:** Security updates can patch vulnerabilities, so make sure your wallet software or firmware is up to date.

6. Consider Using Multiple Wallets

- **Separate Hot and Cold Storage:** For daily transactions, keep only a small amount in a hot wallet and store the rest in cold storage.

- **Divide Large Holdings:** If holding multiple types of assets, consider using separate wallets to minimize risk.

Choosing the Right Wallet Setup Based on Usage

Choosing the right wallet setup depends on your crypto goals, risk tolerance, and access needs:

- **Long-Term Investors (HODLers):** Use a hardware wallet for maximum security. Paper wallets can also be a secure, low-cost option if stored carefully.

- **Active Traders:** Software wallets, especially mobile or desktop wallets, provide quick access for frequent transactions.

- **Businesses or Shared Access:** Multi-sig wallets are ideal for shared control and high-security accounts.

- **Small-Scale or Experimental Users:** Web wallets offer easy access for small balances or experimental use but come with increased risk.

Final Thoughts

A secure wallet setup is the foundation of safe cryptocurrency management. Each wallet type—from hardware to paper to multi-sig—caters to different needs, so consider your security priorities and usage habits before selecting one. By following best practices and staying aware of security risks, you can protect your cryptocurrency from both online and physical threats.

Chapter 7:

How to Buy Cryptocurrency: Exchanges, Platforms, and Secure Purchase Strategies

For beginners, purchasing cryptocurrency can feel overwhelming due to the number of platforms and various buying methods. This chapter provides an in-depth guide to buying cryptocurrency securely, covering different types of exchanges, platform features, step-by-step instructions, and essential security practices that will safeguard your investment. By the end, you'll understand the nuances of purchasing cryptocurrency safely and confidently.

Cryptocurrency Exchanges: Your Gateway to Digital Assets

A cryptocurrency exchange is a digital marketplace where users buy, sell, and trade cryptocurrencies. Similar to stock exchanges, these platforms enable transactions between users while charging fees for their services. Cryptocurrency exchanges can be classified into three main types: **Centralized Exchanges (CEXs)**, **Decentralized Exchanges (DEXs)**, and **Hybrid Exchanges**.

Each type of exchange offers unique features and benefits, making it essential to choose the right one based on your investment goals and security needs.

1. Centralized Exchanges (CEXs)

Centralized exchanges are among the most widely used and accessible platforms for purchasing cryptocurrency. Managed by private companies, CEXs operate similarly to traditional stock exchanges by facilitating transactions between buyers and sellers. Examples of popular CEXs include **Coinbase**, **Binance**, **Kraken**, and **Gemini**.

Key Features of Centralized Exchanges:

- **Fiat-to-Crypto Support:** CEXs make it easy to buy crypto using traditional currencies like USD, EUR, and GBP.

- **Liquidity and High Trading Volume:** With large trading volumes, CEXs offer high liquidity, allowing trades to execute quickly at market rates.

- **User-Friendly Interfaces and Tools:** Most CEXs are designed to be beginner-friendly, offering educational materials, simple buy/sell options, and market analysis tools.

Security Practices on Centralized Exchanges:

While centralized exchanges are the most popular choice for buying cryptocurrency, they are also targets for hackers. Leading CEXs prioritize security through various measures:

- **Cold Storage:** A large portion of user funds is stored offline, or "cold," to prevent unauthorized access.

- **Insurance Policies:** Some CEXs, such as Coinbase, insure user funds in online storage to cover losses due to cyber attacks.

- **Two-Factor Authentication (2FA):** 2FA adds an extra security layer by requiring a one-time code from an authenticator app or SMS in addition to a password.

- **Ongoing Audits:** Top CEXs conduct regular security audits to assess potential vulnerabilities and strengthen defenses.

Pros and Cons of Centralized Exchanges:

Pros:

➤ **Easy to Use:** CEXs are designed with simplicity, making them an ideal choice for beginners.
➤ **High Liquidity:** With large trading volumes, CEXs ensure that trades can be executed with minimal impact on asset prices.
➤ **Wide Range of Coins:** Most CEXs offer hundreds of cryptocurrencies, enabling users to diversify easily.

Cons:

➤ **No Private Key Control:** CEXs are custodial, meaning users don't have full ownership of their assets as the platform holds private keys.
➤ **Potential for Hacking:** The centralized nature makes CEXs a target for hackers.
➤ **KYC Compliance:** To meet regulatory requirements, most CEXs require users to verify their identity, which may feel intrusive for privacy-focused investors.

Examples of Leading Centralized Exchanges:

1. **Coinbase:** Known for its intuitive interface and extensive educational content, Coinbase is a popular choice among beginners, though it has higher fees than some alternatives.

2. **Binance:** Offering a wide range of assets and low fees, Binance is popular with beginners and experienced traders alike, though its advanced features may overwhelm first-time users.

3. **Kraken:** Kraken is known for its security measures and support for various fiat currencies, making it a reliable choice for users worldwide.

4. **Gemini:** U.S.-based and highly regulated, Gemini appeals to users who prioritize security and regulatory compliance.

2. Decentralized Exchanges (DEXs)

Decentralized exchanges are peer-to-peer marketplaces built on blockchain technology, allowing users to trade directly without an intermediary. With DEXs, users retain complete control over their private keys and funds. Examples of DEXs include **Uniswap**, **PancakeSwap**, and **SushiSwap**.

Core Features of Decentralized Exchanges:

- **Non-Custodial Trading:** DEXs enable users to retain control over their funds by holding their private keys.

- **Privacy:** Most DEXs do not require KYC verification, allowing users to trade without disclosing personal information.

- **Automated Market Makers (AMMs):** DEXs use smart contracts and AMM protocols to execute trades, eliminating the need for a central authority.

Benefits of Decentralized Exchanges:

- **User Control Over Funds:** DEXs give users full control of their private keys, enhancing security and reducing custodial risk.

- **Increased Privacy:** DEXs typically don't require identity verification, allowing for more anonymous trading.

- **Open Global Access:** DEXs operate on decentralized networks, making them accessible to anyone with an internet connection.

Drawbacks of Decentralized Exchanges:

- **Lower Liquidity:** DEXs may have less liquidity than CEXs, which can lead to higher price slippage.

- **Higher Complexity for Beginners:** Navigating DEXs can be challenging for newcomers, as they require a working knowledge of wallets and blockchain networks.

- **Transaction Fees:** DEXs on networks like Ethereum can have high gas fees during periods of congestion, making transactions costly.

Examples of Popular Decentralized Exchanges:

1. **Uniswap:** Operating on the Ethereum blockchain, Uniswap allows users to swap ERC-20 tokens and is one of the largest DEXs by trading volume.

2. **PancakeSwap:** Built on Binance Smart Chain, PancakeSwap offers lower fees and fast transactions, appealing to users seeking cost efficiency.

3. **SushiSwap:** SushiSwap provides additional features like staking and yield farming for users interested in decentralized finance (DeFi).

3. Hybrid Exchanges

Hybrid exchanges aim to bridge the gap between centralized and decentralized exchanges by offering both security and user-friendliness. Examples of hybrid exchanges include **Nash** and **Qurrex**.

Core Features of Hybrid Exchanges:

- **User Control Over Funds:** Hybrid exchanges allow users to hold their private keys, reducing custodial risks.

- **Smart Contract Security:** Like DEXs, hybrid exchanges use smart contracts for transactions, though they also provide more intuitive interfaces.

- **Regulatory Compliance:** Hybrid exchanges are designed to comply with regulations but offer greater privacy than traditional CEXs.

Pros and Cons of Hybrid Exchanges:

Pros:

➢ More control over assets while maintaining a user-friendly experience.

➢ Reduced risk of centralized hacking.

Cons:

➢ Lower liquidity than established CEXs.

➢ Limited availability, as hybrid exchanges are still emerging.

Best For: Users who want a mix of security and ease of use, while retaining some control over their funds and privacy.

Key Factors for Choosing an Exchange

Selecting the right exchange is crucial for a secure and efficient trading experience. Here are important factors to consider:

1. **Security:** Choose exchanges with strong security measures like 2FA, cold storage, and insurance coverage.

2. **User Experience:** Beginners benefit from exchanges with intuitive interfaces, educational resources, and responsive support.

3. **Fees:** Compare trading, deposit, and withdrawal fees, as these vary across platforms.

4. **Liquidity:** High liquidity on an exchange ensures you can execute trades quickly and at stable market prices.

5. **Range of Cryptocurrencies:** Ensure the exchange supports your desired coins. Major exchanges offer a wide selection, while smaller ones may focus on niche assets.

6. **Regulatory Compliance and KYC:** DEXs may offer more privacy, while CEXs typically require identity verification for compliance.

Step-by-Step Guide to Buying Cryptocurrency on a Centralized Exchange

Buying cryptocurrency on a CEX is an ideal starting point for beginners. Here's a step-by-step guide:

➢ **Step 1: Choose a Reputable Exchange**

Select an exchange based on factors like security, fees, asset availability, and ease of use. Coinbase and Kraken are good choices for newcomers.

➢ **Step 2: Create an Account and Complete KYC**

Sign up with an email address and password. To comply with regulations, most CEXs require KYC verification, which involves submitting a photo ID and proof of address.

➢ **Step 3: Deposit Funds**

After verification, deposit funds using a bank transfer, credit/debit card, or wire transfer. Processing times and fees vary, so choose a method that suits your needs.

➢ **Step 4: Select Cryptocurrency and Trading Pair**

Navigate to the trading page, select the cryptocurrency you wish to purchase (e.g., Bitcoin), and the fiat trading pair (e.g., BTC/USD).

➢ **Step 5: Place Your Order** Choose from different order types:

- **Market Order:** Executes at the current market price and is ideal for beginners.

- **Limit Order:** Allows you to set a specific price to buy or sell, but it may not execute immediately.

- **Stop-Loss Order:** Automatically sells your asset at a set price to minimize losses.

➢ **Step 6: Transfer to a Secure Wallet**

For long-term storage, move your assets to a private wallet, such as a hardware or software wallet. By controlling your private keys, you ensure your funds are secure.

How to Buy Cryptocurrency on a Decentralized Exchange

For privacy-conscious users, DEXs offer a decentralized, non-custodial method of buying cryptocurrency.

➢ **Step 1: Set Up a Wallet**

To use a DEX, you'll need a compatible wallet like **MetaMask** (for Ethereum) or **Trust Wallet** (for Binance Smart Chain).

➢ **Step 2: Fund Your Wallet**

Transfer a base cryptocurrency like ETH or BNB to your wallet. You can buy these tokens on a CEX and then transfer them to your wallet.

➢ **Step 3: Connect Your Wallet to the DEX**

Visit the DEX's website, such as Uniswap or PancakeSwap, and connect your wallet. No account or KYC is required.

➢ **Step 4: Select Tokens and Initiate Trade**

Choose the token you wish to trade and enter the amount. Confirm the trade in your wallet, ensuring you have enough for gas fees.

➢ **Step 5: Confirm and Pay Gas Fees**

Gas fees are transaction costs on the blockchain. Confirm the transaction in your wallet, and the tokens will appear in your wallet once processed.

Advanced Security Practices for Buying Cryptocurrency

Purchasing cryptocurrency involves certain risks, so following advanced security practices can help safeguard your assets.

Research Coins and Platforms Thoroughly:

Study a cryptocurrency's use case, team, and history before purchasing.

Avoid Emotional Trading:

Crypto prices can be highly volatile, so avoid making impulsive decisions based on price changes.

Diversify to Reduce Risk:

Spread your investments across multiple coins to mitigate risk.

Enable Two-Factor Authentication (2FA):

Use 2FA for extra security, ideally through an app rather than SMS to reduce SIM-swap risk.

Use Secure Wallets for Long-Term Holdings:

Store long-term investments in secure wallets, such as hardware wallets, rather than leaving them on exchanges.

Comparing Payment Methods for Crypto Purchases

Different payment methods have unique fees, processing times, and convenience levels. Here's a comparison:

Bank Transfers: Lower fees but can take several days to process.

Credit/Debit Cards: Instant but usually come with higher fees. Some banks block crypto transactions, so check with your provider.

Wire Transfers: Suitable for large purchases, generally with lower fees but slower processing.

PayPal: Some exchanges offer PayPal, which is convenient but often carries additional fees.

Final Thoughts on Buying Cryptocurrency

Entering the cryptocurrency market is exciting, but it's essential to make informed decisions to ensure a secure experience. By choosing the right exchange, understanding payment options, and following secure buying strategies, you can build your cryptocurrency portfolio with confidence.

Chapter 8:

Analyzing Cryptocurrency Projects: How to Assess Potential Investments

In a rapidly evolving cryptocurrency market, it's essential to approach investments with a structured analysis. With thousands of digital assets available, choosing promising projects can be challenging. In this chapter, we'll go through a comprehensive approach to **fundamental analysis** for cryptocurrency projects, covering aspects like market metrics, technology, tokenomics, team quality, community sentiment, and partnership strength. This method will empower you to identify projects with solid foundations and growth potential while avoiding those with hidden risks or unsustainable models.

The Fundamentals of Cryptocurrency Analysis

Cryptocurrency investing differs significantly from traditional investing. Projects don't typically have cash flow, profit margins, or dividends, so fundamental analysis for cryptocurrency focuses on the purpose of the project, the team's capabilities, the project's long-term viability, and its ability to create value. This means looking beyond price fluctuations and hype to evaluate a project's core attributes and its potential to solve real-world problems.

Key Factors to Evaluate a Cryptocurrency Project

Analyzing a cryptocurrency project requires a multi-faceted approach. Here are the core components to examine, with practical examples and in-depth insights.

1. Market Capitalization, Trading Volume, and Liquidity

Market capitalization is a standard measure of a cryptocurrency's size and stability, calculated by multiplying the coin's price by its circulating supply. However, market cap alone doesn't tell the whole story. Evaluating trading volume and liquidity can provide deeper insights into a coin's resilience and investor demand.

Market Cap Classifications:

Large-Cap Cryptos (Above $10 billion):

Generally less volatile, these cryptos tend to have strong community support and a proven use case.

Mid-Cap Cryptos ($1 billion–$10 billion):

These cryptos are often considered "rising stars," with more growth potential but also higher risk.

Small-Cap Cryptos (Below $1 billion):

High volatility and high risk, small-cap cryptos have a greater chance of dramatic growth or collapse.

Trading Volume and Liquidity:

High trading volume and liquidity are indicators of investor interest and price stability. A high daily trading volume signifies that a coin is popular and can be easily bought or sold, making it less susceptible to drastic price manipulation.

Low Liquidity Warning:

Low-liquidity coins may have high spreads (the difference between buying and selling prices) and are more prone to volatility, as large trades can significantly impact the price.

Practical Example: Ethereum (ETH), with its high market cap, trading volume, and liquidity, is seen as a stable and reliable investment relative to smaller coins. In contrast, a smaller project with low liquidity may experience large price swings if a single investor buys or sells a large volume of the coin.

2. Purpose and Use Case: Addressing Real-World Needs

A cryptocurrency's use case is a primary driver of its value. Successful projects have a clearly defined purpose that addresses a specific problem or offers a unique benefit. In contrast, projects without a clear use case or real-world application often struggle to maintain investor interest.

Analyzing Use Case and Problem-Solving Potential:

Value Creation:

Determine if the project solves an existing problem, adds efficiency, or creates new opportunities.

Market Demand:

Is there a market need for the project's solution? High demand for its utility often indicates a higher chance of long-term viability.

Differentiation and Innovation:

How does the project stand out from competitors? Innovation in technology, scalability, or user experience can create a sustainable competitive edge.

Types of Use Cases and Real-World Applications:

- **Digital Store of Value (e.g., Bitcoin):** Functions as a digital asset that holds value over time and is sometimes compared to "digital gold."

- **Smart Contract Platforms (e.g., Ethereum, Cardano, Solana):** Serve as ecosystems for decentralized applications, offering various use cases in finance, gaming, and supply chain management.

- **DeFi (Decentralized Finance) Tokens (e.g., Aave, Uniswap):** Decentralize traditional financial services like lending, borrowing, and trading, bypassing intermediaries.

- **Privacy Coins (e.g., Monero, Zcash):** Designed for users seeking enhanced privacy and anonymous transactions.

- **Utility Tokens (e.g., Binance Coin, Chainlink):** Used to pay fees or provide services within a specific platform or ecosystem.

Practical Example: Chainlink (LINK) provides decentralized oracle solutions that connect blockchain-based smart contracts with real-world data sources, making it essential for sectors like insurance, finance, and logistics. This specific and valuable use case has contributed to Chainlink's consistent growth and demand.

3. Team, Developers, and Community Contributors: Competence and Commitment

The experience and reputation of a project's team are critical indicators of its potential for success. While cryptocurrency projects don't always have traditional "CEOs" or "managers," their teams still play essential roles in the project's development and adaptation.

Key Factors for Team Evaluation:

- **Industry Experience:** Does the team have experience in blockchain technology, finance, or relevant industries?

- **Reputation and Transparency:** Are the team members publicly known, or is the project led by anonymous developers? Transparency often builds trust, though anonymous teams like that of Bitcoin have succeeded.

- **Commitment and Communication:** Check for regular communication and updates from the team to see if they're actively involved with the project's progress and addressing the community's questions.

Development Team Activity:

Active development is essential to a project's progress. GitHub and similar code repositories reveal the team's commitment to enhancing the project.

Key Metrics on GitHub:

- o **Frequency of Updates (Commits):** Frequent updates show active engagement.

- o **Number of Contributors:** More contributors indicate a wider base of knowledge and potential for growth.

- o **Open Source:** Open-source code promotes transparency, as the community can inspect and contribute to the project.

Practical Example: Cardano's development team is led by Charles Hoskinson, one of Ethereum's co-founders. Cardano's GitHub displays active contributions, and its team consistently communicates through blog posts, social media, and open-source code releases, establishing it as a well-respected project.

4. Whitepaper and Roadmap: Vision, Strategy, and Execution

The **whitepaper** is a project's foundational document. It typically outlines the project's purpose, technical structure, tokenomics, and development goals. A well-written whitepaper can offer crucial insights into the team's level of expertise and the project's scalability.

Evaluating a Project's Whitepaper:

- **Problem Identification and Solution:** Look for a clear problem statement and how the project plans to address it.

- **Technical Soundness:** Does the whitepaper explain the technology in a realistic, feasible way? Complex but understandable technology often indicates a robust approach.

- **Tokenomics and Incentives:** The whitepaper should detail how the token will be distributed, the total supply, and how token holders are incentivized.

Analyzing the Roadmap:

A well-defined roadmap demonstrates a project's strategy for growth and provides milestones that indicate progress. Projects with realistic and achievable roadmaps tend to be better organized.

- **Short- and Long-Term Goals:** Does the roadmap cover the next six months, year, or several years? Short-term milestones show momentum, while long-term goals illustrate the project's vision.

- **Transparency and Accountability:** Projects that publicly update their roadmaps and achieve milestones demonstrate reliability.

Practical Example: Ethereum's whitepaper introduced the concept of a decentralized computing platform with smart contracts, offering a transformative use case beyond cryptocurrency alone. Ethereum's roadmap laid out a multi-phase plan, including the transition to Ethereum 2.0, which demonstrates the team's commitment to scalability and energy efficiency.

5. Tokenomics and Economic Model

Tokenomics is the study of a cryptocurrency's supply, distribution, and incentives. Projects with well-designed tokenomics create a balance between incentivizing users and maintaining token value, while poorly designed tokenomics can lead to inflation, decreased value, and lost investor confidence.

Critical Elements of Tokenomics:

- **Circulating Supply vs. Max Supply:** A fixed max supply, like Bitcoin's, can create scarcity, while projects with no supply limit may experience inflation.

- **Distribution and Allocation:** Token allocation to team members, developers, and early investors can indicate the level of centralization. Projects with highly centralized token ownership are more susceptible to price manipulation.

- **Incentive Mechanisms:** Tokens with built-in rewards, staking opportunities, or governance rights offer additional value to holders and encourage long-term holding.

Practical Example: Uniswap's tokenomics model rewards liquidity providers with UNI tokens, aligning incentives between the platform and its users. This model has made Uniswap one of the leading decentralized exchanges, with a highly active community of liquidity providers and token holders.

6. Development Activity and GitHub Contributions

Tracking a project's **development activity** can reveal insights into its progress, adaptability, and commitment to innovation. Open-source platforms like GitHub enable you to examine a project's codebase, check for regular updates, and assess its developer community's involvement.

Key Indicators on GitHub:

- **Commit Frequency:** Regular updates show ongoing improvement and bug fixes.

- **Number of Contributors:** A larger number of contributors signifies community engagement and a diverse set of skills.

- **Public Accessibility:** Open-source code demonstrates transparency and allows the developer community to provide feedback or contribute.

Practical Example: Ethereum has one of the most active GitHub repositories in the crypto space, with thousands of commits and contributions. This high level of activity reflects Ethereum's adaptability and continual improvement, supporting its dominance in the smart contract sector.

7. Community Engagement and Social Media Presence

A project's community and social media presence can often reflect its popularity, support base, and trustworthiness. The size, engagement level, and sentiment of a project's community can provide valuable insight into its momentum and long-term viability.

Platforms for Community Analysis:

- **Twitter:** Provides updates and announcements, allowing users to gauge overall sentiment.

- **Reddit, Discord, and Telegram:** Offer forums for discussion, often including critical feedback and insights from real users.

- **YouTube and Influencer Support:** Many projects collaborate with influencers, but be wary of paid promotions that create hype without genuine support.

Engagement and Sentiment Indicators:

- **Frequency of Updates:** Projects with consistent updates and communication demonstrate commitment.

- **Authentic Community Support vs. Hype:** Watch for projects with real engagement, where community members ask questions, discuss technology, and share opinions. Excessive hype, fake giveaways, and "moon" promises are red flags.

-

Practical Example: The XRP community, often referred to as the "XRP Army," is known for its active social media presence and strong support base. However, the project has faced regulatory scrutiny, underscoring the importance of balancing community enthusiasm with a thorough assessment of risks.

8. Partnerships and Collaborations: Strategic Alliances

Partnerships with established companies can add credibility to a project, especially when they provide technical support, financial backing, or access to new markets. These partnerships often validate the project's utility and indicate confidence in its long-term potential.

Types of Partnerships:

- **Corporate Collaborations:** Partnerships with prominent corporations or industry leaders indicate credibility and real-world application.

- **Blockchain Alliances:** Collaborations with other blockchain projects, such as interoperability initiatives, can strengthen a project's ecosystem.

- **Institutional Support:** Support from venture capital funds or institutional investors adds credibility and suggests a stable financial foundation.

Practical Example: VeChain's partnerships with Walmart and BMW demonstrate how real-world collaborations can validate a project's use case. By providing supply chain tracking solutions to these companies, VeChain has positioned itself as a valuable tool for logistics and inventory management.

9. Identifying Red Flags and Avoiding Scams

The decentralized nature of cryptocurrency makes it susceptible to scams and fraudulent projects. By identifying red flags early on, you can avoid projects that lack sustainability or have malicious intent.

Common Red Flags to Watch Out For:

- **Promises of Guaranteed Returns:** Be skeptical of projects promising high, guaranteed returns or "get-rich-quick" schemes, as cryptocurrency is inherently volatile.

- **Anonymous Teams with Minimal Transparency:** While not always a dealbreaker, anonymous teams lack accountability, increasing the risk of exit scams or rug pulls.

- **Excessive Hype Without Substance:** Overly aggressive marketing campaigns, celebrity endorsements, or social media "pumps" without a clear use case are red flags.

- **High Token Concentration:** Projects where a few wallets control most of the tokens create risks of price manipulation and sudden dumps.

Practical Example: Many pump-and-dump schemes generate hype by promoting coins aggressively on social media and forums. Once prices are artificially inflated, insiders sell their holdings, leaving late investors with losses. By examining factors like token distribution, purpose, and development activity, you can avoid these types of scams.

Final Thoughts on Analyzing Cryptocurrency Projects

Conducting thorough research and analyzing various aspects of a cryptocurrency project can help reduce investment risk and increase your chances of selecting projects with real potential. By evaluating market cap, use case, team quality, tokenomics, community engagement, and partnership strength, you can make more informed decisions. Remember that all investments carry risk, and cryptocurrency is particularly volatile, so only invest what you can afford to lose.

Chapter 9: How to Store Cryptocurrency Safely: Wallet Types and Security Best Practices

For cryptocurrency holders, **secure storage** is essential. Unlike traditional banking systems, where financial institutions offer protections, the security of your cryptocurrency largely depends on the precautions you take. In this chapter, we'll explore the different types of cryptocurrency wallets, assess each wallet's security profile, and cover comprehensive security practices that can help prevent theft and loss of your digital assets. With these tools and tips, you can keep your cryptocurrency holdings secure and accessible only to you.

The Basics of Cryptocurrency Storage: Understanding Wallets and Keys

Cryptocurrency wallets work through a **public key** (similar to an account number) and a **private key** (like a password). The public key is used for receiving funds, while the private key grants access to your funds and is required to authorize any transactions. Losing your private key can mean losing access to your funds permanently, making private key management one of the most critical aspects of cryptocurrency security.

Types of Cryptocurrency Wallets

Cryptocurrency wallets fall into two main categories: **Hot Wallets** (connected to the internet) and **Cold Wallets** (offline). Choosing the right wallet depends on your security needs, the frequency of access required, and your comfort with various security measures.

1. Hot Wallets

Hot wallets are wallets connected to the internet, enabling easy access for frequent transactions. They are convenient and user-friendly but more susceptible to cyber threats because of their online nature.

Types of Hot Wallets:

1. **Web Wallets**: Hosted by online services or exchanges, accessible via a web browser.

2. **Mobile Wallets**: Applications on mobile devices, useful for on-the-go transactions.

3. **Desktop Wallets**: Software installed on a computer, providing control over private keys while connected to the internet.

Pros of Hot Wallets:

Ease of Access: Ideal for users who need regular access to funds.

Fast Transactions: Provides immediate access to funds, making it easier to buy, sell, or spend cryptocurrency quickly

.

Cons of Hot Wallets:

Increased Vulnerability: Being online makes hot wallets more susceptible to hacking and phishing attacks.

Device Dependency: If the device hosting the wallet is compromised (stolen, hacked, or infected with malware), funds are at risk.

Best For: Users who frequently access or trade cryptocurrency and need convenience.

Practical Example: **Coinbase** or **Binance** web wallets allow users to store funds directly on the exchange. While convenient, it's important to note that the exchange holds the private keys, meaning the user doesn't have full control of the asset's security.

2. Cold Wallets

Cold wallets are offline wallets, making them highly secure against online attacks. They are ideal for long-term storage of large amounts of cryptocurrency and are the preferred choice for users focused on security.

Types of Cold Wallets:

1. **Hardware Wallets**: Physical devices, such as USB drives, that store private keys offline. Examples include **Ledger** and **Trezor**.

2. **Paper Wallets**: A printed document containing both the public and private keys, often generated offline for added security.

3. **Air-Gapped Devices**: Devices completely disconnected from the internet or networks, such as specially prepared laptops or smartphones used solely for managing cryptocurrency offline.

Pros of Cold Wallets:

- **Enhanced Security**: Being offline, they're immune to most types of cyberattacks.

- **Best for Long-Term Storage**: Ideal for "HODLing" (holding assets for long-term gain) due to high security.

Cons of Cold Wallets:

- **Inconvenient for Daily Use**: Requires extra steps to access funds, making them less suitable for frequent transactions.

- **Risk of Physical Loss or Damage**: If the hardware wallet or paper wallet is lost or destroyed, the assets may be irretrievable.

Best For: Long-term investors who want maximum security and do not need regular access to funds.

Practical Example: A **Ledger Nano S** hardware wallet stores private keys offline. When users need to access funds, they connect the device to a computer, enter a PIN, and confirm transactions, adding an extra layer of security.

3. Multi-Signature Wallets

Multi-signature (multi-sig) wallets require multiple private keys to approve a transaction, adding an additional layer of security by distributing control among several parties.

How Multi-Sig Wallets Work: A multi-sig wallet is set up to require multiple parties (keys) to approve a transaction. For example, a 2-of-3 multi-sig wallet would need any two out of three private keys to authorize a transaction.

Pros of Multi-Sig Wallets:

- **Increased Security**: Reduces risk by requiring multiple approvals, preventing single-party access.

- **Ideal for Joint Ownership**: Useful for partnerships or family funds where joint control is needed.

Cons of Multi-Sig Wallets:

- **Complex to Set Up**: Setting up and managing multi-sig wallets can be technically challenging.

- **Slower Transaction Times**: Transactions require multiple signatures, potentially delaying access to funds.

Best For: Businesses or families who want shared access to cryptocurrency funds with an added layer of security.

Practical Example: A business might use a multi-sig wallet with three executives as keyholders. Any two of the three must approve a transaction, preventing unauthorized access while enabling accountability.

Advanced Security Practices for Cryptocurrency Wallets

In addition to choosing the right wallet type, adopting advanced security practices can help protect your assets against unauthorized access, phishing, and even physical theft.

1. Enable Strong Passwords and Two-Factor Authentication (2FA)

Use Complex Passwords: Create passwords with a mix of letters, numbers, and special characters. Avoid using personal information.

Two-Factor Authentication (2FA): Enable 2FA on all wallet-related accounts and exchanges. Use an authenticator app (e.g., Google Authenticator) rather than SMS, as SMS-based 2FA is susceptible to SIM-swapping attacks.

2. Keep Private Keys and Recovery Phrases Secure

Store Keys Offline: Keep private keys and recovery phrases on paper or in a hardware wallet instead of online or in cloud storage, where they could be hacked.

Multiple Backups: Consider creating several backups of your recovery phrases and storing them in secure physical locations (e.g., a safe or safety deposit box).

3. Update Wallet and Firmware Regularly

Software Updates: Wallet software updates fix bugs and vulnerabilities, so ensure you're using the latest version.

Firmware Updates for Hardware Wallets: Regularly update the firmware on hardware wallets (such as Ledger or Trezor) to benefit from the latest security features.

4. Beware of Phishing Attacks

Phishing scams often target cryptocurrency users by mimicking wallet providers or exchanges, attempting to trick users into revealing private information.

- **Check URLs and Email Addresses**: Access wallet sites only through bookmarks or verified URLs, and carefully verify email addresses before clicking any links.

- **Avoid Unverified Applications**: Only download wallet applications from verified sources or app stores to avoid malicious software.

5. Use Dedicated Devices or Secure Operating Systems

For extra security, consider using a dedicated device for cryptocurrency transactions or a secure operating system.

- **Dedicated Device**: Some users designate a specific laptop or phone solely for crypto transactions to minimize exposure to malware.

- **Secure Operating Systems**: Privacy-focused operating systems like **Tails** or **Qubes OS** offer additional security for sensitive transactions.

6. Consider Passphrase Protection for Hardware Wallets

Passphrase Protection:

Hardware wallets often offer an optional "passphrase" feature, which adds an extra layer of security. Even if someone gains physical access to your wallet, they would need this additional passphrase to access your funds.

Practical Example: On a **Ledger Nano** device, you can add a passphrase as an extra PIN. This feature makes it harder for unauthorized users to access your wallet, even if they have the physical device.

Physical Security Tips for Wallets and Backup Storage

Since many wallets, particularly cold wallets, involve physical components, it's important to secure them against physical threats as well.

1. Store Hardware Wallets and Backups in Secure Locations

Use Safes or Lockboxes:

Store hardware wallets, recovery phrases, and backups in a secure location such as a safe or lockbox. This prevents unauthorized physical access and protects against potential home intrusions.

Paper Wallets and Metal Wallets:

For paper wallets, use a waterproof, fireproof storage container to guard against physical damage. Metal wallets, which engrave recovery phrases on stainless steel or titanium plates, are another durable option.

2. Backup Using Durable Materials (Metal Wallets)

Metal Wallets: Metal wallets, such as **Cryptosteel** or **Billfodl**, are fireproof, waterproof, and resistant to corrosion. By engraving or securing your private keys or recovery phrase on metal, you protect them from physical hazards like fire, water damage, and aging paper.

Practical Example: Using a Cryptosteel capsule to engrave your recovery phrase on metal plates ensures that your backup remains intact even in extreme conditions.

3. Use Multiple Backup Copies and Locations

Distribute backup copies across multiple locations to reduce risk. For example, you might store one backup in a home safe, another in a trusted relative's safe, and a third in a safety deposit box. This ensures that even if one backup is compromised, you retain access to your assets.

Common Mistakes to Avoid in Cryptocurrency Storage

Avoiding common pitfalls can greatly enhance your cryptocurrency security:

1. **Leaving Funds on an Exchange**: Storing cryptocurrency on an exchange is convenient but risky. Exchanges are frequent targets for hackers. Transfer significant holdings to a private wallet.

2. **Weak Passwords or Reused Credentials**: Using simple or repeated passwords can put your funds at risk. Use a password manager if needed.

3. **Failure to Enable 2FA**: Two-factor authentication (2FA) is a simple and effective security measure, so make sure to enable it on every exchange or wallet where it's available.

4. **Forgetting to Make Backup Copies**: Without backup copies of your recovery phrases, you risk permanently losing access to your wallet if the device is lost or damaged.

5. **Sharing Sensitive Information**: Never share your private key or recovery phrase, even with people claiming to be "support" for your wallet or exchange.

Choosing the Right Wallet Setup Based on User Needs

Selecting the appropriate wallet setup depends on your investment goals, how often you need access, and your security priorities.

1. **Long-Term Holders (HODLers)**: Use a hardware wallet, such as a Ledger or Trezor, for maximum security. For very high-value holdings, consider a multi-sig wallet or additional passphrase protection.

2. **Frequent Traders**: A hot wallet on a trusted exchange, combined with a secure mobile wallet, offers quick access while keeping a portion offline.

3. **Shared Access (Business or Family)**: Multi-sig wallets provide added security, ideal for users needing shared or limited access.

4. **Casual Users**: For small amounts or casual use, a mobile wallet like **Trust Wallet** or **Exodus** is convenient and secure.

Final Thoughts on Cryptocurrency Storage and Security

Protecting your cryptocurrency assets requires a layered approach, combining the right wallet, advanced security practices, and constant vigilance. By using appropriate storage methods and following the security practices outlined in this chapter, you can significantly reduce the risks associated with holding digital assets.

Chapter 10:

Buying Cryptocurrency Safely: Choosing Exchanges, Payment Methods, and Transaction Tips

Entering the world of cryptocurrency starts with your first purchase, and doing so safely is essential. This chapter will guide you through selecting a secure exchange, comparing payment methods, and executing transactions safely. By understanding these elements, you can buy cryptocurrency with confidence and protect your assets from common risks.

Understanding Cryptocurrency Exchanges

A **cryptocurrency exchange** is a digital marketplace where users can buy, sell, and trade various cryptocurrencies. Think of it as similar to a stock exchange but for digital currencies. Each exchange offers unique features, fee structures, and security protocols, so selecting the right one requires thoughtful consideration.

Types of Cryptocurrency Exchanges

1.Centralized Exchanges (CEXs):

Managed by private companies, centralized exchanges (CEXs) provide a user-friendly interface, secure infrastructure, and high liquidity. Examples include **Coinbase**, **Binance**, **Kraken**, and **Gemini**.

Pros:

- **Liquidity**: High trading volumes make buying and selling fast and efficient.

- **Fiat Support**: CEXs support fiat currency deposits, making it easy to buy crypto directly with cash.

- **User-Friendly**: Beginner-friendly interfaces, customer support, and resources for new investors.

- **Advanced Features**: Large exchanges often offer trading tools, margin trading, staking, and lending options.

Cons:

- **Custodial Nature**: CEXs hold your private keys, reducing user control over funds.

- **KYC Compliance**: CEXs often require identity verification (Know Your Customer, or KYC), which may compromise privacy.

- **Hack Risk**: Due to their centralized structure, they are prime targets for hackers.

2.Decentralized Exchanges (DEXs):

Decentralized exchanges operate without an intermediary, allowing users to trade directly with each other. DEXs are typically non-custodial, meaning users retain control of their private keys. Examples include **Uniswap**, **PancakeSwap**, and **SushiSwap**.

Pros:

- **User Control**: Users keep control of their private keys, enhancing security.

- **Privacy**: No KYC requirements, preserving user anonymity.

- **Decentralized Structure**: Reduces the risk of a single point of failure and hack incidents.

Cons:

- **No Fiat Support**: DEXs generally do not support fiat-to-crypto conversions, so users must already own cryptocurrency to trade.

- **Complex Interface**: DEXs are less intuitive, which can be challenging for beginners.

- **Lower Liquidity**: May experience slippage or higher price fluctuations.

3.Hybrid Exchanges:

Hybrid exchanges aim to combine the best of CEXs and DEXs by offering user control over private keys while maintaining a user-friendly interface and liquidity. Examples include **Nash** and **Qurrex**.

Pros:

- **Balance of Control and Usability**: Hybrid exchanges provide both security and ease of use.

- **Privacy with Compliance**: Complies with regulatory requirements without compromising user privacy.

Cons:

- **Limited Options and Liquidity**: Hybrid exchanges are still emerging and may have lower liquidity and fewer trading pairs than larger CEXs and DEXs.

Practical Tip: If you're new to crypto, starting with a reputable centralized exchange like **Coinbase** or **Kraken** offers ease of use and support for fiat transactions. As you become more experienced, consider exploring DEXs for more privacy and control.

Evaluating a Cryptocurrency Exchange

Choosing an exchange involves assessing its security measures, reputation, and overall reliability. Here are the critical factors to evaluate:

1.Security:

Security should be your top priority when choosing an exchange. Look for exchanges with multi-layered security features, including:

- **Two-Factor Authentication (2FA)**: Adds an extra layer of security by requiring a second form of verification (such as an app-based code).

- **Cold Storage**: Reputable exchanges store a majority of assets offline to minimize hacking risks.

- **Encryption**: Protects user data and transaction information from unauthorized access.

- Regular Audits: Exchanges that conduct regular security audits demonstrate a commitment to safeguarding user funds.

- Red Flags: Avoid exchanges with a history of hacks or weak security practices. Publicly available security reports, transparency about past breaches, and compensation policies can also reflect an exchange's security commitment.

2.Reputation and Track Record:

Research an exchange's background, paying attention to user reviews, online feedback, and any regulatory issues.

- Reliable Platforms: Platforms like Kraken and Gemini are known for high compliance standards and strong security records.

- Avoid Platforms with Frequent Incidents: Exchanges with unresolved hacking issues, sudden fund freezes, or frequent customer service complaints may not be reliable.

3.Supported Cryptocurrencies:

Confirm that the exchange offers the cryptocurrencies you intend to purchase. While most support popular assets like Bitcoin and Ethereum, some also offer niche altcoins.

Fees: Exchanges charge various fees, including:

- Trading Fees: Usually a percentage of each trade (e.g., Binance charges 0.1% for spot trading).

- Deposit and Withdrawal Fees: Vary depending on payment methods and currency types.

- **Network Fees**: These apply to withdrawals and are paid to miners or validators rather than the exchange itself.

- **Fee Comparison**: Some exchanges, like **Binance**, offer relatively low trading fees, while others, like **Coinbase**, charge higher fees for simplicity and user-friendliness.

4.Customer Support:

Accessible customer support is invaluable, especially for beginners. Look for exchanges with live chat, phone, or email support and positive feedback on response times.

Practical Example: If you're looking for a secure and beginner-friendly exchange, **Coinbase** may be a suitable choice despite higher fees. If you prioritize low fees and access to a wide range of cryptocurrencies, **Binance** is another strong option, though it may be less intuitive for beginners.

Payment Methods for Buying Cryptocurrency

Each exchange supports different payment options, each with its pros and cons. Here's a breakdown of the most common methods:

1.Bank Transfer (ACH or Wire):

Most exchanges support ACH (Automated Clearing House) or wire transfers, offering a low-fee option for buying cryptocurrency.

 Pros: Low fees, typically free for ACH transfers; suitable for larger purchases.

Cons: Processing times can be slow, ranging from a few hours to several business days, especially for international wires.

2.Credit or Debit Card:

Many exchanges accept credit and debit card payments, allowing for quick and easy purchases.

Pros: Instant access to funds, convenient for beginners.

Cons: High fees (often 3-5% per transaction); some banks may block crypto purchases.

3.PayPal:

Select exchanges, such as **Coinbase** and **eToro**, support PayPal as a payment method.

Pros: Fast and convenient, especially for users with existing PayPal accounts.

Cons: High fees and limited availability (offered only by specific platforms and in certain regions).

4.Peer-to-Peer (P2P) Transfer:

P2P platforms, like **LocalBitcoins** or **Paxful**, allow users to buy crypto directly from other individuals, often with flexible payment options.

Pros: Privacy, variety of payment methods, including bank transfers, cash, and gift cards.

Cons: Higher risk of fraud; requires careful vetting of buyers and sellers.

Practical Tip: Bank transfers are typically the most cost-effective option, especially for large purchases. However, for quick transactions, using a credit/debit card may be worth the added fees if you need instant access.

Step-by-Step Guide to Buying Cryptocurrency on a Centralized Exchange

For most beginners, buying cryptocurrency on a centralized exchange offers a secure and straightforward experience. Here's a step-by-step guide:

1. **Choose an Exchange and Register**:

   Select a reputable exchange like Coinbase or Kraken. Register an account using a secure email and create a strong password. Many exchanges require two-factor authentication (2FA) for added security.

2. **Complete Identity Verification (KYC)**:

   To comply with regulations, exchanges often require Know Your Customer (KYC) verification. This typically involves uploading a government-issued ID, a photo of yourself, and sometimes proof of address.

3. **Deposit Funds**:

After verification, deposit funds using your preferred payment method (such as a bank transfer or credit card). Processing times and fees will depend on the chosen payment method.

4. **Select a Cryptocurrency and Trading Pair**:

   Choose the cryptocurrency you wish to purchase (e.g., Bitcoin) and select its trading pair (e.g., BTC/USD for Bitcoin against the U.S. dollar).

5. **Choose an Order Type**:

   o **Market Order**: Executes immediately at the current market price. It's simple but may not offer the best price.

   o **Limit Order**: Executes when the cryptocurrency reaches a specified price, offering more control over the trade.

   o **Stop-Loss Order**: Automatically sells your asset if the price drops to a set level, helping to prevent major losses.

6. **Transfer Funds to a Private Wallet**:

   For added security, transfer your funds to a private wallet, such as a hardware wallet. Storing significant assets on an exchange exposes them to potential risks, as exchanges are frequent hacking targets.

Practical Example: Suppose you're buying Ethereum on Coinbase. After depositing funds via bank transfer, go to the ETH/USD pair, select a market order, confirm the transaction, and transfer your ETH to your private wallet for secure storage.

Step-by-Step Guide to Buying Cryptocurrency on a Decentralized Exchange (DEX)

For users who prioritize privacy and control over their assets, decentralized exchanges (DEXs) are a suitable choice. Here's how to buy cryptocurrency on a DEX:

1. **Set Up a Non-Custodial Wallet**: Download a wallet app like **MetaMask** (for Ethereum) or **Trust Wallet** (for Binance Smart Chain). This wallet allows you to retain full control of your private keys.

2. **Fund Your Wallet**: Transfer a base cryptocurrency (e.g., ETH or BNB) to your wallet. You can buy this on a CEX and transfer it to your DEX wallet.

3. **Connect Your Wallet to the DEX**: Visit the DEX's website (e.g., Uniswap) and click "Connect Wallet." You won't need to create an account, as DEXs operate directly through your wallet.

4. **Choose Your Tokens and Trading Pair**: Select the token you want to buy and the base currency you'll use. Enter the amount and review the transaction details.

5. **Confirm and Pay Gas Fees**: Transactions on blockchains like Ethereum require gas fees (paid in ETH). Confirm the transaction in your wallet and pay the necessary gas fee.

Practical Example: To buy a token on Uniswap, connect your MetaMask wallet, select the token, enter the amount, confirm the transaction, and pay the gas fees. Once confirmed, the tokens will appear in your wallet.

Best Practices for Buying Cryptocurrency Safely

Following best practices can help you minimize risks and protect your investment. Here are some essential tips:

1. **Verify URLs and Use Official Apps**: Phishing attacks are common in crypto. Only use official exchange websites and verify the legitimacy of apps before downloading.

2. **Enable Two-Factor Authentication (2FA)**: Enable 2FA on all exchange accounts for an additional security layer.

3. **Avoid Public Wi-Fi for Transactions**: Public Wi-Fi networks are vulnerable to hackers, so use a private, secure network for crypto transactions.

4. **Start Small**: If you're new to crypto, start with small purchases to familiarize yourself with the process before making larger investments.

5. **Be Wary of Scams**: Learn about common scams in the crypto world, such as fake exchanges, phishing schemes, and Ponzi schemes. If something seems too good to be true, it probably is.

Comparing Payment Methods Based on Transaction Needs

Different payment methods are better suited to different types of transactions. Here's a quick comparison:

- **Large Transactions**: Bank transfers are low-cost and suitable for large transactions, though slower processing can be a drawback.

- **Instant Access**: Credit and debit cards are ideal for small, quick purchases but may involve higher fees.

- **Privacy**: Peer-to-peer (P2P) platforms provide privacy and flexibility but require careful verification of sellers/buyers.

Practical Example: For larger investments in Bitcoin, a bank transfer is usually cost-effective and safe. For smaller, instant buys, using a debit card can be convenient, provided you're aware of the associated fees.

Final Thoughts on Buying Cryptocurrency Safely

Purchasing cryptocurrency is your entry point into the digital economy, and it's essential to do so safely. By selecting reputable exchanges, choosing appropriate payment methods, and following best practices, you can minimize risks and protect your assets. Remember to transfer your funds to a secure private wallet for long-term storage, keeping your investment safe from external threats.

Chapter 11:

Evaluating Cryptocurrency Projects: How to Analyze Market Potential, Risks, and Opportunities

With thousands of cryptocurrency projects in the market, selecting the right one for investment requires a strategic approach and careful assessment. Unlike traditional assets, many cryptocurrencies lack consistent financial data, so evaluating them involves understanding their technology, use case, economic model, and more. This chapter provides a structured method to analyze cryptocurrency projects, helping you to identify solid opportunities while avoiding high-risk ventures.

Overview: Why Evaluating Cryptocurrency Projects is Different

In traditional investments, financial metrics like revenue, profit margins, and dividends provide insight into a company's health and growth. Cryptocurrencies, however, often lack such metrics, requiring investors to focus on other aspects. The key factors for crypto analysis include **technology**, **tokenomics**, **real-world applicability**, **community support**, **partnerships**, and **regulatory considerations**. This evaluation process helps determine if a project has a sustainable, value-driven future or if it's simply riding on hype.

Key Factors to Evaluate a Cryptocurrency Project

1. Market Capitalization, Liquidity, and Trading Volume

Market capitalization (or market cap) provides a quick look at a project's size and significance. It's calculated by multiplying the current price of the cryptocurrency by its circulating supply. Generally, higher market cap projects are more stable and have stronger market trust, whereas smaller projects may offer higher rewards but come with increased risk.

- **Large Market Cap (Over $10 Billion)**: Typically represents well-established projects like **Bitcoin** and **Ethereum**. High market caps are associated with market stability and established user trust.

- **Mid Market Cap ($1 Billion–$10 Billion)**: Mid-cap assets like **Cardano** and **Polkadot** carry moderate risk, offering potential growth as they gain traction.

- **Small Market Cap (Under $1 Billion)**: Small-cap projects, such as **VeChain** or **Basic Attention Token**, often provide high growth potential but come with higher volatility and liquidity concerns.

Liquidity is essential for avoiding price slippage when trading, as it indicates how easily an asset can be bought or sold without significantly impacting its price. Higher liquidity generally means more stable prices and easier trading. For example, **Bitcoin** and **Ethereum** have very high liquidity, making them more stable in comparison to smaller projects.

Trading Volume indicates how actively a cryptocurrency is traded, which in turn reflects demand and market interest. High trading volumes are desirable, as they show investor confidence and make it easier to enter and exit positions.

Practical Example: Bitcoin's large market cap, high liquidity, and consistent trading volume make it a popular choice for conservative investors, while a smaller project like **Basic Attention Token (BAT)** may appeal to those seeking potential high-growth opportunities at a higher risk.

2. Use Case and Real-World Applications

A project's **use case** is one of the strongest indicators of its potential for sustained demand. Cryptocurrencies with clear, real-world applications often have better adoption rates, helping them achieve long-term value.

Evaluating Use Cases:

- **Problem Identification**: Look for projects that solve a real problem. For example, **Ethereum** supports smart contracts, providing a foundation for decentralized applications (dApps).

- **Market Demand**: Projects with high market demand and clear applicability tend to attract user adoption and investor interest. For instance, **Chainlink** addresses a need for reliable data oracles, making it essential for decentralized finance (DeFi) platforms.

- **Innovation and Competition**: Projects offering unique solutions or innovations stand out. **Polkadot**, for example, focuses on cross-chain interoperability, which sets it apart in the blockchain space.

Types of Use Cases:

1. **Digital Currency**: Cryptocurrencies like Bitcoin serve as a decentralized alternative to traditional currencies, functioning as a store of value or medium of exchange.

2. **Smart Contract Platforms**: Platforms like Ethereum and Cardano enable dApps and programmable contracts, creating a foundation for various decentralized services.

3. **Privacy Coins**: Coins like Monero focus on secure, private transactions, addressing concerns over anonymity and security in financial transactions.

4. **Utility Tokens**: Tokens like Binance Coin provide value within a specific ecosystem, enabling reduced fees or access to services on that platform.

Practical Example: Ripple (XRP) aims to streamline cross-border payments for financial institutions. By partnering with banks and payment providers, Ripple has created a unique use case, adding real-world value beyond speculation.

3. Team and Development Activity

A project's **team** and developer community are pivotal to its success. Projects with experienced, transparent teams are more likely to deliver on their promises, while active development signals ongoing commitment and innovation.

Assessing the Team:

- **Background and Expertise**: Teams with experience in blockchain, finance, or tech industries are often better equipped to execute a project's vision.

- **Transparency**: Transparent, public teams inspire trust. Anonymous teams may lack accountability and pose a higher risk of "exit scams."

- **Developer Community**: Look for active developer involvement on platforms like GitHub. An open-source repository allows investors to track development frequency, contributions, and code quality.

Evaluating Development Activity:

Consistent updates, regular code commits, and project enhancements reflect the project's health. Low activity could indicate a lack of progress, while steady development often signals a project's long-term viability.

Practical Example: **Cardano's team**, led by Charles Hoskinson, regularly updates the community about development progress, creating a transparent and trustworthy relationship with investors. Cardano's GitHub activity also shows high engagement, demonstrating the team's commitment.

4. Whitepaper and Roadmap

The **whitepaper** and **roadmap** are essential documents for understanding a project's goals, technology, and planned development. Reviewing these documents provides insight into the project's potential and its commitment to a clear vision.

Evaluating a Whitepaper:

- **Problem and Solution Clarity**: A strong whitepaper clearly states the problem the project addresses and how it will solve it. If the explanation is overly complex or vague, it may indicate a lack of focus.

- **Technical Specifications**: Look for technical details that explain how the project will achieve its goals. Overly technical language without real substance can be a red flag.

- **Tokenomics**: The whitepaper should outline the token's purpose, distribution, and any incentives for holding or using the token.

Assessing the Roadmap:

- **Milestones and Goals**: Projects with clearly defined milestones demonstrate strategic planning. Key milestones, such as mainnet launches, upgrades, or partnerships, indicate the project's growth trajectory.

- **Adherence to Deadlines**: A project that meets its milestones on schedule shows effective planning and execution.

Repeated delays or lack of transparency about setbacks can indicate management issues.

Practical Example: **Polkadot's whitepaper** clearly explains its interoperability solution, while its roadmap outlines crucial milestones, like parachain integration and ecosystem expansion, showcasing a strong commitment to development.

5. Tokenomics and Economic Model

Tokenomics refers to the design of a token's economic model, which includes its supply, incentives, and distribution. Strong tokenomics can help a cryptocurrency achieve sustainable demand and value growth.

Key Components of Tokenomics:

- **Supply and Scarcity**: Limited-supply tokens, like Bitcoin, have inherent scarcity, which can drive demand. Tokens with inflationary models need to ensure sustainable issuance rates to avoid devaluation.

- **Distribution**: A fair distribution model ensures that tokens are widely spread rather than concentrated in a few wallets, reducing manipulation risks.

- **Incentives and Utility**: Tokens with functional value, like staking rewards or governance rights, encourage engagement and long-term holding.

Practical Example: **Uniswap's UNI token** incentivizes liquidity providers and enables holders to participate in protocol governance, creating alignment between user engagement and the project's goals.

6. Community and Social Media Presence

A strong, active **community** can amplify a project's success, helping to drive adoption, provide feedback, and spread awareness. A healthy community typically indicates solid support for the project's mission.

Evaluating Community Engagement:

- **Platform Activity**: Look at platforms like Twitter, Reddit, and Telegram for community activity. High engagement often reflects strong user interest.

- **Sentiment Analysis**: A constructive and positive community is a good indicator, whereas excessive hype or fanfare without substance could be a red flag.

- **Organic Growth**: Authentic engagement is preferable to artificially generated hype through influencers or bots.

Practical Example: **Ethereum's community** is known for active engagement, educational content, and ongoing discussions, supporting Ethereum's development and creating long-term interest in the project.

7. Partnerships and Collaborations

Strategic **partnerships** add credibility and provide valuable resources for a project. Collaborations with established companies or blockchain projects can help a cryptocurrency reach broader markets and build user trust.

Types of Partnerships:

- **Corporate Collaborations**: Partnerships with corporations validate a project's real-world use case. For instance, Ripple's partnerships with banks and financial institutions underscore its goal of improving cross-border payments.

- **Blockchain Partnerships**: Collaborations with other blockchain projects can expand a project's ecosystem and enable interoperability.

- **Institutional Investments**: Institutional backing from venture capital firms or large asset managers indicates experienced investors see value in the project.

Practical Example: **Chainlink's partnerships** with Google, Oracle, and major DeFi platforms highlight its utility in connecting smart contracts to real-world data, making it a vital part of the DeFi ecosystem.

8. Regulatory Compliance and Legal Standing

Regulatory compliance is critical in the evolving cryptocurrency landscape. Projects that are transparent about their regulatory approach are generally more secure and less likely to face legal issues.

Evaluating Regulatory Compliance:

- **Jurisdiction**: Projects based in crypto-friendly regions (e.g., Switzerland, Singapore) often enjoy more regulatory clarity and protection.

- **Compliance Transparency**: Projects that adhere to KYC (Know Your Customer) and AML (Anti-Money Laundering) regulations are better positioned to operate in regulated markets.

- **Risk of Regulatory Action**: Projects that operate in legally ambiguous areas or avoid regulatory scrutiny face significant risks of shutdowns or legal action.

Practical Example: **Coinbase's compliance with U.S. regulations** has allowed it to grow into one of the most widely used exchanges, while projects that avoid regulation often face greater uncertainty.

9. Red Flags and Potential Scams

The decentralized nature of cryptocurrency makes it vulnerable to scams. Identifying potential red flags can help avoid projects with weak fundamentals or malicious intent.

Common Red Flags:

- **Guaranteed Returns**: Cryptocurrencies are highly volatile, and projects promising guaranteed profits are typically scams.

- **Anonymous Team**: Projects with anonymous or pseudonymous teams lack accountability and pose a higher risk.

- **Excessive Marketing and Hype**: Be cautious of projects that rely more on hype and celebrity endorsements than technology or development.

- **High Token Concentration**: Projects where a few wallets hold a large percentage of tokens are vulnerable to manipulation and sudden price drops.

Practical Example: Many "pump-and-dump" schemes rely on aggressive marketing to inflate a token's price, only for insiders to sell at a peak, leaving retail investors with significant losses. Authentic projects focus on substance rather than hype.

Final Thoughts on Evaluating Cryptocurrency Projects

Evaluating cryptocurrency projects requires a thorough analysis of technical, financial, and strategic factors. By examining aspects like market cap, use case, team, partnerships, and compliance, you can make informed investment decisions, maximizing growth opportunities while minimizing risks.

Chapter 12:

Building a Balanced Cryptocurrency Portfolio: Diversification, Risk Management, and Long-Term Strategies

Investing in cryptocurrency can be both thrilling and challenging. While the potential for high returns exists, so do significant risks. Crafting a well-diversified, carefully managed portfolio is essential for navigating this volatile landscape. In this chapter, we'll explore how to diversify across asset classes and use cases, employ advanced risk management techniques, and implement long-term strategies to achieve stable and sustainable growth.

Why a Balanced Cryptocurrency Portfolio is Essential

Unlike traditional markets, the cryptocurrency market is marked by high volatility and rapid innovation. A balanced portfolio enables investors to spread risk across different assets and sectors, avoiding overexposure to any single project. Additionally, strategic diversification and risk management protect your capital from market downturns while capitalizing on the growth potential of emerging assets.

An effective portfolio consists of a blend of stable, high-value assets and smaller, high-growth assets. By managing risk effectively and implementing a disciplined, long-term strategy, you can create a resilient portfolio that performs well across various market conditions.

Step 1: Diversifying Your Cryptocurrency Portfolio

Diversification reduces risk by spreading your investments across multiple assets, industries, and sectors. In the cryptocurrency market, diversification involves selecting assets with varying use cases, market caps, and growth potentials.

Types of Cryptocurrencies for Portfolio Diversification

1. **Large-Cap Coins**: Large-cap coins, such as **Bitcoin (BTC)** and **Ethereum (ETH)**, are the foundation of most crypto portfolios. They offer lower volatility than smaller assets, high liquidity, and a strong market presence. Bitcoin is often seen as a store of value, while Ethereum is known for its smart contract functionality and DeFi ecosystem.

2. **Mid-Cap Coins**: Mid-cap assets, like **Polkadot (DOT)**, **Solana (SOL)**, and **Chainlink (LINK)**, provide growth opportunities with moderate risk. These coins often represent more established projects with solid use cases, such as interoperability or data oracles. Mid-cap coins can enhance a portfolio's growth potential without adding excessive risk.

3. **Small-Cap Coins**: Small-cap coins, including newer DeFi tokens, emerging dApp platforms, or niche projects, offer high-risk, high-reward potential. Small caps can be highly volatile, with the potential for rapid gains but also significant losses. Due to their speculative nature, they should represent a smaller portion of the portfolio.

4. **Stablecoins**: Stablecoins, like **USDT (Tether)**, **USDC (USD Coin)**, and **DAI**, maintain a peg to fiat currency (usually the USD), providing stability and acting as a hedge during market volatility. Stablecoins also facilitate easy reallocation within the portfolio and act as a cash reserve for purchasing assets during market downturns.

5. **Alternative Blockchain Platforms**: Alternatives to Ethereum, such as **Avalanche (AVAX)** and **Cardano (ADA)**, often focus on high-speed, low-fee transactions. These platforms aim to improve upon Ethereum's functionality, making them strong options for diversification within smart contract platforms.

6. **NFT and Metaverse Tokens**: With the rise of NFTs and the metaverse, tokens like **Decentraland (MANA)**, **Axie Infinity (AXS)**, and **The Sandbox (SAND)** offer exposure to digital assets that cater to gaming, digital real estate, and virtual economies. These assets provide unique diversification within the crypto market, driven by consumer interest and industry partnerships.

Practical Example: A diversified portfolio might include 35% in Bitcoin and Ethereum for stability, 25% in mid-cap assets like Polkadot and Chainlink, 10% in small-cap coins with growth potential, 20% in stablecoins for stability, and 10% in NFT/metaverse tokens to capture growth in emerging digital asset classes.

Diversifying Across Use Cases and Sectors

Diversifying by use case ensures your portfolio is not overly reliant on any single segment within the cryptocurrency market. This approach allows you to capture growth across various sectors, mitigating the impact if one sector faces regulatory scrutiny or technological setbacks.

1. **Store of Value**: Assets like Bitcoin are often viewed as digital gold, serving as a hedge against inflation and market volatility.

2. **Smart Contract Platforms**: Platforms such as Ethereum, Solana, and Cardano support dApps, making them essential to DeFi, gaming, and NFT applications.

3. **Decentralized Finance (DeFi)**: Projects like **Uniswap (UNI)**, **Aave (AAVE)**, and **Curve (CRV)** facilitate decentralized lending, borrowing, and trading. DeFi projects are innovative but come with higher regulatory risks.

4. **Privacy Coins**: Privacy-focused coins, such as **Monero (XMR)** and **Zcash (ZEC)**, appeal to users who prioritize anonymity, adding a layer of privacy to the portfolio.

5. **Oracles**: Chainlink (LINK) and Band Protocol (BAND) are critical for providing external data to blockchain applications, particularly in DeFi.

6. **NFT and Metaverse Tokens**: Projects like Decentraland (MANA) and Axie Infinity (AXS) offer exposure to virtual economies and digital asset ownership within virtual worlds.

Practical Example: A diversified portfolio by sector could consist of 30% in smart contract platforms, 20% in store-of-value assets like Bitcoin, 20% in DeFi tokens, 10% in oracles, 10% in stablecoins, and 10% in NFT/metaverse tokens.

Step 2: Advanced Risk Management Techniques

Due to the high-risk nature of cryptocurrency, managing risk is essential. Advanced risk management techniques help protect your capital and keep you from taking excessive risks that could impact your portfolio's stability.

1. Position Sizing

Position sizing is the allocation of specific percentages of your portfolio to different assets based on their risk levels. It's essential to balance larger positions in safer, large-cap assets and smaller positions in riskier, speculative assets.

- **Larger Positions in Stable Assets**: Allocate a significant percentage of your portfolio to assets like Bitcoin and Ethereum, which have lower volatility and high liquidity.

- **Smaller Positions in Risky Assets**: High-risk assets, such as small-cap tokens or highly speculative projects, should be limited to a smaller percentage of your portfolio to mitigate potential losses.

Practical Example: If you're investing $10,000, you might allocate $5,000 to Bitcoin and Ethereum for stability, $3,000 to mid-cap projects, and $2,000 across small-cap projects to capture growth potential without overexposure.

2. Implementing Stop-Loss and Take-Profit Orders

Stop-loss and take-profit orders are automated trades that activate when an asset reaches a specified price, helping you lock in profits or limit losses.

- **Stop-Loss Order**: Set a stop-loss to automatically sell if the price drops to a specified level, protecting you from large losses.

- **Take-Profit Order**: Set a take-profit order to secure gains when the asset reaches a target price, preventing you from holding through potential downturns.

Practical Example: If you purchase Solana at $100, setting a stop-loss at $85 would limit potential losses to 15%, while a take-profit at $130 would secure a 30% gain.

3. Dollar-Cost Averaging (DCA)

Dollar-cost averaging (DCA) reduces risk by investing a fixed amount at regular intervals rather than all at once. DCA is effective in volatile markets, allowing you to buy assets at different price points and reducing the impact of market swings.

- **Regular Interval Investments**: Invest a set amount each week or month, smoothing out your purchase prices over time.

- **Avoiding Market Timing**: DCA is particularly useful for long-term strategies, as it avoids the need to time the market perfectly.

Practical Example: Instead of investing $5,000 in Bitcoin in a single transaction, investing $500 monthly over 10 months can help you accumulate Bitcoin at an averaged price, reducing exposure to market peaks.

4. Portfolio Rebalancing

Portfolio rebalancing involves adjusting the asset allocation in your portfolio to maintain your intended diversification. Rebalancing allows you to take profits from assets that have appreciated and reinvest in assets that may be undervalued.

- **Periodic Review**: Assess your portfolio every three to six months to determine if any adjustments are necessary.

- **Reallocating Gains**: If a particular asset has grown disproportionately, consider selling a portion to rebalance and reinvest in other assets or stablecoins.

Practical Example: If Bitcoin grows to represent 60% of your portfolio after a bull market, you might sell some Bitcoin to reduce it to your original allocation of 40%, using the proceeds to rebalance into mid-cap assets or stablecoins.

5. Hedging with Stablecoins and Asset Rotation

In volatile markets, converting part of your portfolio into stablecoins can help preserve value. Stablecoins like USDC or DAI act as a safe harbor, providing liquidity for quick purchases when prices dip.

- **Stablecoin Rotation**: In a bear market, rotating volatile assets into stablecoins can prevent losses.

- **Reallocation During Dips**: Holding stablecoins gives you the flexibility to reallocate into growth assets during market downturns, allowing you to buy assets at lower prices.

Practical Example: If your mid-cap tokens experience a 50% increase, rotating part of your gains into USDC allows you to protect profits while maintaining flexibility for future investments.

Step 3: Long-Term Cryptocurrency Investment Strategies

Long-term investment strategies promote disciplined and goal-oriented investing. These approaches focus on sustainable growth rather than short-term gains, which is crucial in the volatile world of cryptocurrency.

1. HODLing for Long-Term Growth

HODLing (holding onto assets long-term, regardless of market fluctuations) is a common strategy for assets expected to appreciate over time, like Bitcoin or Ethereum.

- **Focus on Blue-Chip Cryptos**: Large-cap assets like Bitcoin and Ethereum are well-suited for HODLing, as they benefit from community support and long-term growth potential.

- **Weathering Volatility**: HODLers avoid selling during market dips, focusing on long-term appreciation instead.

Practical Example: Buying Bitcoin at $30,000 and holding it for five or more years regardless of price drops is a HODL strategy aimed at capturing long-term growth.

2. Yield Farming and Staking for Passive Income

Yield farming and **staking** generate passive income by lending or staking assets within DeFi platforms, earning rewards that compound your holdings over time.

- **Yield Farming**: Providing liquidity on decentralized exchanges like Uniswap can earn you a share of transaction fees.

- **Staking**: Platforms like Cardano or Ethereum 2.0 allow staking, where you can earn additional tokens for locking your holdings in the network.

Practical Example: Staking Ethereum 2.0 can yield 4-8% annually, compounding your holdings without requiring active trading.

3. Value Averaging: Dynamic Investment Allocation

Value averaging involves setting a target growth amount and adjusting your contributions based on whether the asset meets that target. This technique requires more active management but can yield higher returns than standard DCA.

- **Adjusting Contributions**: If an asset underperforms, increase your contribution; if it outperforms, reduce or sell part of the asset.

- **Enhanced Flexibility**: Value averaging adapts to market conditions, allowing you to buy low and sell high systematically.

Practical Example: If your monthly goal is to increase your Bitcoin position by $500, you would invest more if the price drops or less if the price increases, stabilizing growth while adapting to market fluctuations.

4. Seasonal Market Cycles and Allocation Adjustments

Cryptocurrency markets often exhibit cyclical trends. Seasonal reallocation involves adjusting your holdings to capitalize on these trends, such as increasing exposure to small caps in bull markets and shifting to stable assets in bear markets.

- **Bull Market Adjustments**: In bullish cycles, you might increase exposure to high-growth assets, like small-cap DeFi tokens.

- **Bear Market Adjustments**: During bearish cycles, rotating into stablecoins or large-cap assets like Bitcoin can provide stability.

Practical Example: In a bull market, increasing exposure to smaller DeFi tokens can capture upside potential, while in a bear market, reallocating into Bitcoin or stablecoins preserves capital.

Summary: Building a Resilient Crypto Portfolio

Creating a resilient cryptocurrency portfolio involves thoughtful diversification, proactive risk management, and disciplined long-term strategies. By balancing large-cap assets with growth assets and speculative investments, managing risk through tools like stop-losses and DCA, and using strategies like HODLing and staking, you can achieve sustainable growth while protecting against volatility.

Remember, patience, consistency, and regular portfolio reviews are essential to managing a cryptocurrency portfolio. As you grow more comfortable, refine your approach to adapt to the market and stay aligned with your financial goals.

Legal Disclaimer

This book is intended for informational and educational purposes only. The author has made every effort to ensure the accuracy of the information provided; however, this book should not be considered as financial, legal, or investment advice. Cryptocurrency markets are highly volatile and involve significant risk. Always conduct your own research and consult with qualified financial or legal professionals before making any investment decisions.

The author and publisher expressly disclaim any liability for any losses or damages incurred as a result of using this book, either directly or indirectly. No guarantee of future results is implied or expressed, and past performance is not indicative of future outcomes.

By reading this book, you agree that the author and publisher are not responsible for your investment decisions, and you assume all responsibility for any outcomes.